The Life Diet

The Life Diet

Live Long, Live Lean, & Maximize Your Potential

Dr. Chace Unruh

No Limit Publishing Group
123 E Baseline Road D-108
Tempe AZ 85283
info@nolimitpublishinggroup.com

This book was printed in the United States of America

No Limit Enterprises, LLC
1601 E 69th Street, Suite 200
Sioux Falls, SD 57108

Contents

"And so, my fellow Americans, ask not what your country can do for you; ask what you can do for your country."

— **John F. Kennedy**

Dedication

To Jackson, Truman and Monroe

The joy you have each brought to my life is immeasurable. You have allowed me to work tirelessly on this and many projects for the development of others. You have given me the ability to serve others to a larger capacity with this book and I pray you inherit the same passion I have towards servitude and pass it on to the next generation of Americans.

To Cassidy

Wow, you should be given the woman of the century award. You have allowed me to serve and educate others with no complaining and even when it's been extremely tough your sacrifice and dedication to our family is and will always be unconscionable to me. Thank you for your commitment to me. As you know over the years I have devoted my life to helping and growing others, while in the mist of it all you have helped me grow with your infinite wisdom. I enjoy every second we have together and can't wait to see what the next 60 years will bring. I love you.

YOUR RIDDLE

I am your constant companion.
I am your greatest helper or your heaviest burden.
I will push you onward or drag you down to failure.
I am at your command.
Half of the tasks that you do you might just as well
Turn over to me and I will do them quickly and correctly.
I am easily managed,
You must merely be firm with me.
Show me exactly how you want something done;
After a few lessons, I will do it automatically.
I am the servant of all great people and
Alas of all failures as well.
Those who are great I have made great.
Those who are failures I have made failures.
I am not a machine, but I work with all the precision
Of a machine, plus the intelligence of a person.
Now you may run me for profit or
You may run me for ruin.
It makes no difference to me.
Take me, train me, be firm with me
And I will lay the world at your feet.
Be easy with me and I will destroy you.

Who am I?

Chapter 1

Your First Step to Wellness

"I have to have an adjustment before I go into the ring. I found that going to a chiropractor three times a week helps my performance. The majority of boxers go to get that edge."

—Evander Holyfield
Professional Boxer

Define Wellness

On a daily basis, we are bombarded with the term "wellness." However, how many of us actually take a minute to reflect on what it means and why it is so important? Contrary to what muscle magazines and diet ads may have you believe, this term does not only apply to the physical aspect of your being, but rather encompasses a trinity that includes mind, body, and soul. The wellness of your mind can be described as your conscious attitude as well as your mental capacity to reflect on the positive aspects of life rather than the negative. The wellness of your body consists of factors such as proper nutrition, a well balanced diet, and regular exercise, while wellness of the soul encompasses your spiritual life and philanthropic endeavors.

In order to be a truly successful and a "well" human being, you need to give each of these three aspects equal priority rather than just focusing on one or two of them. There are some people who exercise their bodies five hours a day, take all the right supplements, but don't invest the time to develop their mental or spiritual well-being. Alternatively, some believe that through prayer or positive thinking alone "things will fall into place," and tend to neglect the physical aspect of their being, never taking positive action steps to achieve goals. Extremes are never healthy, and often lead to negative results. The most successful people are those who understand the importance of balancing their entire mind, body, and spirit. You can go into the office and be super successful, making huge deals, but if at home you are faced with the constant struggle for balance, your body and soul will suffer, and, in the long run, your success level will drop drastically.

Do we ever become fully well or is wellness infinite?

Some people view wellness in the same light as they view financial success—as a "get rich quick scheme." The internet is full of opportunities to earn millions in a very short period of time, with the promise of never having to work another day in your life. Those who go on crash diets, cram for tests, and go to church only once a year tend to view wellness in the same manner. In reality, get rich quick schemes never work, and neither do crash diets. Wellness is something that takes effort to maintain on a daily basis. You cannot train for just one marathon and expect to be able to maintain that same level of stamina without an effective training regimen.

The same goes for spirituality, your connection to your soul and God. These connections must be acknowledged on a daily basis rather than just once a year. You need to expand your mind by opening it to new ideas and challenges on a daily basis, rather than assuming that as soon as you get out of school you have completed your education. Wellness is a lifelong process. Your goal should be to put forth consistent effort to attain it and work hard at maintaining it in order to reap the full benefits of a balanced life.

Why should I strive to be well?

Striving to be well pulls the mind away from misery and hopelessness and turns you toward happiness and joy. Making a daily effort to make the very best choices for your own body, and for those in your care, produces a feeling of accomplishment and purpose that creates a momentum that determines the direction of your life. Remember that small actions lead to bigger ones, and years are made up of days. The sum of your life is only a compilation of small decisions. We all want a good life, full of promise and purpose! When we are in a state of wellness, we tend to make better decisions, wouldn't you agree?

When was the last time you made a great decision while under stress or a severe lack of sleep? Striving for wellness is neither an empty pursuit nor a shallow one. It is simply a matter of having enough wisdom and perspective to recognize the value in it and build it into your daily life. Your whole family will benefit from having a dad or mom who is more even tempered and patient, who has invested a bit of time into wellbeing and who isn't reduced to a mere shadow of themselves at the end of a long day. This happens to all of us at times, but with a bit of forethought and planning, it is avoidable most of the time.

Remember, you are also setting an example for the children in your home. When you strive to be well, you show them that it is valuable to exercise the body, to feed it nourishing things, to give it enough rest, and to take time to laugh as well. These children then have a much better chance at a balanced life because they have seen its principles practiced in their home.

People who strive to be well have few regrets about their lives. On the other hand, a 40 year old with lung cancer likely has tremendous regret about choosing to smoke. If you choose to neglect one aspect of your well-being, you will definitely feel the effects of it in a profound way, whether immediately or in the future. For instance, not eating properly will have a severe impact on your physical health, so you will never truly be able to achieve your true potential on a mental or spiritual level. Your whole life will be in conflict, preventing you from achieving goals that you may have set for yourself.

Where You Are

Why do I need to determine where my current results are in my wellness?

Determining your current results is like using a tape measure to see if you have lost inches on your waist or hips. If the tape shows a lower number, you know you have made progress; if it shows a higher number, you know that you need to make further changes. If you have no idea where you are starting from, you will walk around in circles rather than moving forward.

"Everything that is happening at this moment is a result of the choices you've made in the past."

— Deepak Chopra, MD

Many people make the same New Year's resolution every year, to lose those ten pounds. What they don't realize is that over the course of the holidays they most likely put on 10 pounds, so even if they lose 10 pounds, they haven't made any real progress! If you take the time to measure your current status, you can gauge whether you are moving forward, going backward, or standing still. Without measuring results, you choose to maintain a façade of wellness rather than actually striving for wellness.

Once you accept your current position, you can begin to accept your failures and faults to avoid self-delusion and move forward. For instance, if you are taking a supplement for better health and see that it is not working for you, you can accept that fact and try another one. Once you are brave enough to admit past failures, future success becomes easier.

In which areas of my life do I need to measure my results?

There are four primary areas on which we should all focus when measuring our results. These areas are *family, work, social,* and *spiritual.* If you make time for family and respect each member, chances are your home life will be peaceful and well balanced. On the other hand, if you're constantly fighting with your spouse and your children are always fighting with you and each other, you know something needs to be examined and readjusted.

In your work life, you can gauge your results from examining how happy your employees or coworkers are. You need to ask yourself if your employees are happy and thankful to work with you or if they are resentful. In my practice, I make sure my employees are happy by offering rewards for productivity as well as taking an interest in what is important to them. The tone of a doctor's office is determined by the personality of the professionals who work there. If they are temperamental and cold, the office will be tense and employees will be on edge. What's the mood/tone of your workplace?

Make an effort to make room for your friends. Nourish your social life. Take the time to stop and smell the roses, because when everything is said and done, every aspect of your life comes into play, not just one at a time. You can work hard and save all the money in the world, but on your deathbed the sum in your bank account should be the last thing on your mind. If you can spend enough time on work without neglecting family and friends, and still take time to recharge yourself, chances are you are on your way to a beautiful, balanced life!

Where You Want to Be

Why is it important for me to set goals for my wellness?

You need to set goals to move forward. There is absolutely no way around it. If you don't set goals and make plans to move ahead, chances are you will become frustrated with your circumstances, get bored, give up, and eventually end up disappointed in yourself and depressed. Imagine hopping on the freeway and trying to drive from San Francisco to New Orleans without any road signs, map, or GPS. To most people, any task without a goal is impossible because they have no idea where they are headed. When you have a map, you have direction, and from there you can determine where you are going.

"I am not there yet, but I am closer than I was yesterday."

— Anonymous

In life, there are seasons. Each season holds the potential for a new goal or project or purpose. What is your goal for this season? What are your goals for this year, month, and week? Ask yourself what you want to achieve during this decade, and discover which direction you need to go in order to achieve your goals. Make it a priority to focus on others rather than solely on yourself and your own aspirations. Volunteer at your church, synagogue, or local charity. Spend some time with your kids doing what they enjoy, ask your spouse what you can do to lighten his or her load today. The more you help others, the further you will be from misery and self-pity when things aren't going just right. Being "happy" can be a surface emotion, but true joy and balance come only from giving and serving others. Thrive and get through hard times. Don't let lack of personal goals hold you back.

How will this help me today?

Put simply, setting goals will give you purpose and clarity. This purpose is both for today and for the rest of your life. Goals add excitement to daily life; they bring on emotions, enthusiasm, drive, and motivation. For instance, in football simply running around with a ball and crashing into people seems pointless until a touchdown is made. That exact moment in which the ball crosses the goal line brings on emotions and clarity as to why all of that effort was needed in the first place. When I set goals I do so with the near future in mind and I think in terms of six months or at maximum five years while setting any goal. Life is bigger than just that so you have to think in the short and long term. If you want to achieve something magnificent out of your life, you have to set goals accordingly so that during your life you always are in perspective.

Visualize yourself being 90-95 years old and you are at the end of your life. What do you think your achievements should be? What would make you happy at this age? You want to say that you didn't leave any stone unturned, or in other words don't want to leave anything on the table. By doing this you will figure out the motivational factors for your life.

Lifestyle Centered on Wholeness

Wholeness can be defined as a state of completeness in which nothing more is needed. When you are whole, nothing needs to be added because you are not missing anything, and all the pieces of your life are in alignment. When you feel complete in terms of family, friends, work, and the state of your soul, prosperity will follow.

The word wholeness has power to awaken a personal desire within all of us. We all long to be whole person. Don't you? Don't you want to accomplish what you were designed for, having all the ingredients of your personality expressed in balance, or in other words true wholeness? We are all so aware of our own shortcomings, of our lack of wholeness. We know how much we hurt ourselves and each other. Many people have difficulty coping with their lives. This would be a mark for lack of wholeness. We also know our diabolical power to irritate, to enrage, and to inflame others. This again is another indication that we are not whole. Once you can identify some of the things that will keep you from being whole, it is easier to stay on track and on the road to a life centered around "true wholeness."

What are three steps to help me live in wholeness?

1. **Create and execute healthy habits**: Healthy habits promote wellness rather than destroying wellness.

2. **Don't dilute your purpose**: When you dilute your purpose, you lose focus, and this leads to a loss of motivation and failure to meet your goals.

3. **Discipline yourself to take the road less traveled**: Most people choose the path of least resistance, the easy way. Most things that are worth doing don't come easily, so when they do come, you appreciate them all the more. Make smart food

choices, not the easy ones; take the stairs when possible; go to church regularly. To strengthen your most important relationships, play silly games with your family or turn off the TV occasionally. Read a challenging, interesting, or instructional book or just take a walk and resist trying to do everything at once!

Identifying Potential Hurdles

If you know where pitfalls are, you can navigate around them easily. If you know that someone has a negative impact on your mood and causes you to react in a questionable manner, you should do your very best to avoid interacting with him or her. If, after a long day, you are given to low blood sugar and irritability due to hunger, make it a point to prepare for that situation in the morning by preparing a healthful snack for after work and storing it in your car for the drive home. Your loved ones should look forward to your daily homecoming, not hide out until they know the coast is clear. Identify potholes and hurdles in every aspect of your life so you can learn from previous experiences. If you don't learn from history, it will repeat itself.

" All problems become smaller if you don't dodge them, but confront them."

— William F. Halsey

Ask yourself: what are my weaknesses and strengths? Ask trusted loved ones the same question. Once you identify these traps and pitfalls, you will gain the insight to avoid negative situations whenever possible.

Identify healthy habits and core disciplines

Have you figured out the answer to the riddle at the beginning of the book yet?

The answer is:
I am a Habit.

Webster's Dictionary defines habits as "the prevailing disposition or character of a person's thoughts and feelings; makeup."

Habits can be either constructive or destructive, so it is critical to separate the good from the bad. Seemingly innocent actions such as having a drink or two after work can quickly develop into a bad habit, and worse. Behaviors that are not aligned with wellness can be defined as bad habits. If you know you have a certain habit that is negative, you need to distance yourself from it, whether it is relational, emotional, or physical. Over time, your goal should be to establish positive habits.

Wrong habits can take down nations. We will never know some of the greatest men and women in history because they had bad habits and lacked the discipline to change them. So many people with amazing minds choose to be destructive instead of productive. They develop negative habits and ways of thinking that handicap their potential.

Once you focus on habits that create wellness, you will be able to address the areas in your life that demand change. Once you start making positive changes, everything becomes easier. Foster good habits. If you want to get into shape, you need to make a point to get up in the morning, take a supplement, and engage in a daily exercise routine. View your alarm clock as an "opportunity clock." These little changes in mental observations will help you achieve these goals and turn them into good habits.

What is discipline relative to wellness?

Discipline allows you to focus on those habits that are healthy so they become easier and allow you to achieve your goals. If you don't have the correct level of discipline, you're going to fail. If a ship loses engine power, nothing keeps pushing it forward. If you lose discipline, nothing drives you to challenge yourself. Unless you are in control of your own destiny, you will never reach your wellness goals because you have no clarity in any area of your life. You must have strong discipline to stay focused and form the habits to reach your goals. If you don't have correct habits, it is easy to lose control. Remember that all areas of your life go hand in hand.

Identify those things in life that drive you, so you can go forward into total prosperity. Eliminate the negativity from your life wherever possible, and remember that there are people in situations that are much worse than your own. You need to be accountable for your own actions and stop making excuses for what happened to you in the past. People who are not disciplined enough to move forward and take ownership of their future will remain in a cycle of bitterness about their past. Always put things in perspective. You will never get total joy out of life unless you are willing to work for it. Contrary to popular belief, happiness is not served on a silver platter. You need to make a conscious effort to be happy.

Chapter 2

The Wellness Lifestyle

"I got a chiropractor to come along to the patriot shoot, because they can actually stick you back together within 5 minutes. He spent a week and worked on the entire crew. All the stunt guys were like, 'Oh, fix my disc.' It was amazing."

—Mel Gibson, Actor

The Wellness Lifestyle

THE WELLNESS LIFESTYLE is a state of optimal conditions for normal function. This is not about popping pills to get a quick fix, but rather requires the close examination of underlying causes of any disturbance that may be afflicting your body. It is only after these factors are located and properly dealt with through necessary interventions and lifestyle adjustments that you can begin the path to a lifestyle centered on wellness.

When the body is working properly, it tends to heal effectively, no matter its condition. When the body heals well and maintains itself well, then it reaches another level of health that reveals an open-ended opportunity for vitality, vibrant health, and an enhanced experience of life. Optimal living is a choice you must consciously make in order to attain a state of being that allows you to excel in all other areas of your life.

How does one go about achieving a higher level of being? Optimal living can be achieved first by understanding that your body can only run as effectively as the quality of ingredients you put inside that body. Good nutrition is the key to all other facets of your being. Unfortunately, our society makes it all too easy to opt for short-term pleasures that are full of cancer-causing preservatives, colors, and artificially enhanced flavors. These foods may give you a quick boost, but in the long run they will only cause harm to your body. There is an undeniable connection between faulty nutritional habits and disease. Yet so many people still choose to buy whichever product has the fattest advertising budget.

Flashy gimmicks and promises of calorie-reduced meals are more popular than ever. However, with the proper education you can learn how to separate good food choices from bad. Learning how to read food labels is like looking at a prescription for your health and your life. Just about every packaged food made in the U.S. has a food label indicating serving size and other nutritional information. The "Nutrition Facts" food labels give you information about the specific packaged food in question, including measurements of fat, cholesterol, sodium, carbohydrate, protein, vitamins, and minerals. These terms and concepts are often confusing due to the fact that we are flooded with incorrect information on a routine basis, so it is important to be well informed.

You can make sure you are well educated by reading reputable books as well as consulting experts in the field, such as a qualified holistic nutritionist. Once you understand the importance of good nutrition and start applying its principles to your own lifestyle, you will be renewed. You will eliminate the physical ailments bad nutrition brings with it such as headaches, fatigue, and loss of mental clarity, and become a more productive individual.

What are the three (3) most critical habits I need to adopt in order to truly live well?

Affirmations can be described as positive self-talk designed to help you create the life of your dreams.

Using affirmations on a daily basis is a simple step you can take to get what you want out of life and to reduce stress, fear, and depression. Repeating positive, affirmative statements to yourself will change your self-image, raise your self-esteem, and forge an attitude of expectancy. Most people consistently struggle with believing that they are good enough. The truth is if you don't tell yourself you are good enough, you never will be good enough. In order to create confidence and attract abundance into your life, you need to have faith in your own abilities. Without confidence, there is no excellence and no room for personal growth.

Here are some keys that will allow you to maximize the power of your daily affirmations:

- Write affirmations down. This allows you to crystallize your thoughts and gives you a reference to refer back to daily.

- Affirmations should be in the first person and in the present tense. They should always contain the word "I" and be in the "now" time frame, as they are the truth, told in advance.

  Remember the rule: "To Become, Act As if."

- Affirmations are best done in the morning to start your day or in the evening before going to sleep. Reprogram your mind to focus on what makes you feel confident.

- Affirmations can be memorized or read, and must be said aloud with emotion. This is necessary to open the door between your educated and innate mind. **Attitude**, or how you perceive the world around you, makes all the difference. People are drawn to things that give us pleasure and reduce our pain and suffering. Naturally, most of us do not want to be around people who drag us down with their negativity. If you have a good attitude, you can impact those around you in a positive manner while striving towards your own goals. For instance, if you are faced with adversity, but choose to handle it with class and move forward, you automatically become an inspiration. Examine your own life. Are people attracted to you? Are they turned off? Does the manner in which you carry yourself inspire others? Do you have that "Wow Factor?" Are people drawn to you without explanation or do you always have excuses for your problems? Just remember, attitude is everything. When you don't have a good attitude, people are not going to be drawn to you. If you find yourself around toxic people who drag you down, it is okay to distance yourself. Choose to live on your own terms. Negative emotions are powerful and destructive forces that need to be kept at bay. In order to be safe, it is best to remove yourself completely from their path.

Daily planning and preparing to win on an everyday basis is a must.

Long-term goals are important but not many people take the time to reflect on them throughout the course of a year. More often, New Year's resolutions are made and then quickly forgotten. This makes them pointless. In order to ensure that your life is not pointless, you need to take baby steps on a daily basis. For example, if weight loss is your goal, then don't say that you are going to lose 25 pounds and forget about it. Actually lose 25 pounds by making a conscious effort every day. Wake up in the morning and exercise, don't go to the supermarket on an empty stomach or stuff your face with pizza before bed. If you stay positively focused on baby steps, you will eliminate your chances of failure. In order to succeed in whatever you take on, you need to be prepared. Success doesn't happen by pure luck. It happens through planning.

The proper perspective as to your body

Only you have the power to decide whether your body is a temple or a trash can. Studies have proven that life requires nurturing care. Plants and infants respond well to classical music and tend to go in the opposite direction when exposed to destructive music. Keeping this in mind, it is safe to assume that everything to which you expose your body has an impact on your well-being. If you seek a body that is going to live for a hundred years, you need to feed it with only the purest ingredients as often as possible.

"Don't compromise yourself.
You are all you've got."

— Betty Ford

If you see your body as a temple, you will begin treating it as one. Start treating your body like an expensive Porsche rather than an old, beat up Pinto. Once you start viewing your body as your most valuable and expensive asset, you will start investing in it. Investing in your body means making time for wellness and striving for excellence. Instead of delaying goals, take small steps every morning to improve your state of being. If you want to lose weight, set the alarm for 5 a.m. and hit the gym. Avoid eating sugary foods throughout the day and stick to fruits and vegetables, lean proteins, and complex carbohydrates.

Like the ancient pyramids, your body is unique and cannot be replicated. You need to be good to yourself and love yourself before you can make any positive impact on the world around you. You cannot inspire greatness unless you first strive for it yourself. Quit making excuses. If you want to do something, believe you can achieve it. As Americans, we have all the advantages in the world, yet so many people cling to petty excuses and reasons why they cannot do something. They choose to be held down by their circumstances rather than overcome their limitations. Statistics indicate that the growing numbers of millionaires in America are immigrants rather than American born: "Nine of the richest Americans added to this year's Forbes 400 are distinguished by the fact that they were not born in this country. With a collective net worth of $20.5 billion, it's easy to see why talented foreigners have their sights set not only on American colleges and universities, but also the seemingly limitless opportunity and access to capital that's often not available elsewhere." [1]

Why is this? As a society, we are so spoiled that we have forgotten how to work for what we want. Compared to other nations, everything is handed to us on silver platter, yet we fail to realize it. In order to stop making excuses and realize your full potential, you need to start with yourself. Treat your body with the respect it deserves so you can stop making excuses and start striving for excellence.

Wellness Care vs. Sick Care

What's the main difference between wellness care and sick care? Wellness care seeks to activate the natural healing ability, not by adding something to the system, but by removing anything that might interfere with normal function, trusting that the body knows what to do if nothing interferes with it. Sick care, on the other hand, seeks to treat a symptom by adding something from the outside—a medication, surgery, or procedure.

For instance, if a patient has high blood pressure, the standard medical approach would be to choose a drug that lowers blood pressure, and ask the patient to take the drug

1   (DiCarlo).http://www.forbes.com/finance/lists/54/2000/immigrants.jhtml?passListId=54&passYear=2000&passListType=Person

indefinitely. This may serve to lower the blood pressure, but ignores the underlying cause that is making the blood pressure high and runs the risk of side effects complicating the person's recovery. Some of those side effects are depression, weight gain, diabetes, heart failure, fatigue, and dizziness.[2] Some may have lower blood pressure after taking the drug but now have multiple other medical issues from the drug. Whether it's a nutritional issue, faulty nervous system control, or a manifestation of stress, the medication could decrease the blood pressure, leaving the root problem causing the symptom of high blood pressure unaddressed.

Once you commit to a lifestyle that revolves around wellness care rather than sick care, the veil of excess noise and static that clouds your vision will be lifted. You will no longer live life in a foggy, dreamlike state in which events happen to you. Instead, you will be able to dictate your own narrative and become the author of your own book. Telling your own story empowers and motivates you to be more proactive in every area of your life.

"Too much of a good thing can be wonderful."

— Mae West

---

2   http://www.lipitor.com/

Most people have no idea what goes into their bodies on a daily basis but rather rely on the Food and Drug Administration to tell them what is acceptable or unacceptable. As children, most of us couldn't wait to break away from our parents and claim our independence, yet as adults we continue to rely on strangers to make life or death decisions on our behalf. This makes no sense. Make your own decisions by becoming educated and doing your own research. Of course, pharmaceutical companies are going to advise you that drug X is necessary or drug Y will improve your condition, but this is because they run on profit. Sadly, the sicker you are, the happier they are. Don't let these corporations profit from your pain. Food additives are there for only one reason, to save money, or in other words to generate profit. If you're not dead, you don't need to preserve your body with chemicals, but with all the preservatives people are consuming on a daily basis, you would think the opposite. Do you want to die early to save nameless, faceless billionaires a few pennies? Don't compromise your body and your health. Take a step back and examine the type of lifestyle you are living. Adopt the 100-year plan and make healthy choices.

Three (3) major benefits of wellness care:

1. **Increased energy levels**: Once you embrace a lifestyle centered on wellness, your energy levels will increase and your aches and pains will disappear. Eating well and exercising on a daily

basis allow your body to remain in top form so you won't be blindsided by sudden illness.

2. **Mental clarity**: Choosing to live well allows you to connect with your spiritual side by giving you the gift of mental clarity. Without noise clouding your vision you will be able to connect better with those around you as well as with your inner spirit.

3. **Empowerment**: Choosing wellness empowers you to take control of your own life. As a society, we allow others to make decisions for us too often. Make a conscious decision to live an excellent lifestyle. Be proactive by picking up a book and going to a nutritionist. More and more people on medications choose to not to be a statistic and embrace a natural diet. Remember that short-term fixes only lead to long-term problems. Take control and put yourself in the driver's seat.

Chapter 3

True Wellness

---

*"Live with intention. Walk to the edge.
Listen hard. Practice wellness. Play with
abandon. Laugh. Choose with no regret.
Appreciate your friends. Continue to
learn. Do what you love. Live as if this
is all there is."*

—Mary Anne Radmacher

True Wellness

THE TERM "WELLNESS" HAS RECENTLY become quite the buzzword in today's society. Unfortunately, in my opinion, the word wellness is also being grossly misused. For example, being a healthcare provider in Southern California, I get many health-related advertisements, via e-mail and/or in direct mail. One of these is a local magazine advertiser which claims to be a wellness guide. They put a couple of basic articles about vitamins or exercise together and then fill the rest of the magazine with articles and advertisements from cosmetic surgeons, cosmetic dentistry, beauty salons, tanning parlors, etc. In other words, this magazine's definition of wellness is what you look like on the outside. It is not uncommon for celebrities, athletes, models, etc., to undergo very unhealthy procedures or practices in order to improve their appearances. So they look good, but is looking good wellness? The medical profession also misuses the term wellness in many of their programs, promotions, and advertisements. The medical model of wellness care, sometimes called preventive care, is based on the population receiving annual checkups, heart scans (blood pressure, heart rate, cholesterol, EKG), mammograms, prostate exams, colonoscopies, pap smears, and diabetes screenings, just to mention a few. Important tools? Absolutely. Do any of these exams or screenings really create health or wellness? Obviously not. The medical community is simply trying to take advantage of the popularity of the new wellness movement by making us think that "early detection" leads to true wellness. Early detection will and can prevent a particular disease from spreading but it isn't wellness.

> *"Whenever I had a little problem with my body, I always ran to one of my dear friends, who is a chiropractor. He was always right there with the adjustments. This is how I found out the best way of going, is to use chiropractors, not only after injuries, but also before injury."*

> **—Arnold Schwarzenegger, Former Actor and Governor of California**

So what exactly is true wellness? According to The New Oxford American Dictionary, wellness is "the state or condition of being in good physical and mental health."

True wellness means having all the pillars in this book working together to give you life goals and true clarity. There is no magic pill or vitamin that instantly leads to good health. You have to be financially well, develop yourself spiritually, move your body through exercise, and proactively seek out practitioners who can help you invest in your health. Chiropractors (like me) are just some of the many practitioners who can help you achieve true, lasting wellness in the form of structural care.

We can only create true wellness through our lifestyle choices. Is your lifestyle moving you toward true wellness or away from it?

What is chiropractic?

Chiropractic is the art and science of movement. It focuses on the removal of nerve interference as well as the restoration of corrective movement. The primary focus of this field is to remove those things that interfere with the body's natural, normal healing ability. Restoration allows the body to function at its peak without any further wear and tear to the joints. Any irritation on a nerve or fiber doesn't allow your body to function at its fullest. You may start off by losing as little as 10% of your nerve function, but this can translate into severe dysfunction over time, and may manifest in the form of ulcers or organ malfunction. Many patients come in for an adjustment and instantly feel better in general rather than just one particular area. This feeling of relief stems from the body being completely healthy and in balance.

"Pain is inevitable. Suffering is optional."

—Anonymous

Chiropractic is the art and science of naturally removing nerve interference to restore corrective joint function. If joints continue to function in an unnatural way, they begin to break down and interfere with the body's ability to function normally.

Chiropractic is not:

Chiropractic is not some sort of religion or cult. There is no dark mystery behind how it works and the relief derived from it is not magical. It is simple physiological law. In *Bone Pathology*, Wolf states that "bone remodels stress." When you place repeated stress on a joint, the bone will be remodeled by the buildup of bone deposits in the joint spaces. This leads to the narrowing of the joint, which results in pain due to inflammation.

To put it in simple terms, if something is not moving correctly, it will remodel. On the other hand, if your joints are moving freely, you won't see any changes but you will feel a major improvement in how your body feels. These are facts people tend to overlook when considering chiropractic treatment options. Before jumping to conclusions, it is critical to do your own research and discover why so many patients seek out this treatment. If there were no benefits to chiropractic care, insurance companies would not cover the costs, but most do. These companies understand that it makes a difference and is necessary so they are willing to insure patients.

If a patient walks though my office doors and says, "I don't really believe in this," I ask if he or she believes in gravity. Just as the existence of gravity is a proven fact, the manner in which chiropractic functions is also a proven fact.

How does it work?

I recently sat down to lunch with a neurosurgeon friend of mine and he asked me this question. He said that he didn't take Chiro 101 in medical school and told me that he doesn't see any evidence of subluxation (bone out of place) in the spine when he operates on someone's spine. He told me he had seen amazing results from chiropractic but wanted to understand how it worked. The problem I told him was in the misunderstanding of what a subluxation is. It's not a dislocated joint complex; it's a lot more complex than that. So I will describe in detail the answer to this question.

First we have to understand a few terms. Segmental Dysfunction (AKA "Vertebral Subluxation Complex"): A vertebral segment consists of two adjacent vertebral bones, a disc to separate and cushion the bones, muscle, tendons, and ligaments to stabilize and move the joint and a segment of the spinal cord with nerve roots that branch off that segment. When you have a dysfunctional segment this means one or more of the components of the vertebral segment are not working properly, and affects the entire segment. Segmental dysfunction most notably affects the nerve roots that emerge from each side of the segment. These nerve roots carry important information to and from the muscles and organs throughout the body. Dysfunction of the L4-L5 vertebral segment, for example, can cause pain or weakness in the leg and may also affect the bladder.

Basic symptoms of segmental dysfunction can manifest themselves in many different ways. It is possible to have segmental dysfunction and experience no symptoms for weeks, months, or even years. In the later stages of this process, the most common symptoms are back pain, neck pain, headaches, numbness/tingling in the arms or legs, shoulder pain, arm pain, and leg pain. Segmental dysfunction can also be linked to reproductive problems, bowel and bladder problems, problems in the circulatory system, sinus problems, eye, ear, nose, and throat problems, and so on.

What causes segmental dysfunction? Sometimes this condition is idiopathic, meaning we can't really trace it back to a certain accident or activity. Some of the common known causes are trauma, degenerative disc disease, dysafferentation (a neurological term), ligamentous sprain, muscular strain, thoracic outlet syndrome, disc prolapse, flat feet, mental stress, and many others. Dysafferentation is really the reason behind the "miracle" of chiropractic. To understand this term we need to understand a little neurology. There are two kinds of nerves that come from the spinal cord; afferent nerves that carry information from the body to the brain, and *efferent* nerves that carry information from the brain to the body. So, dysafferentation refers to faulty signals being sent to the brain from somewhere in the body. In most cases I see, these faulty signals are coming from the spinal muscles. There are two types of muscle in the spine: superficial and deep. The superficial muscles are the larger muscles close to the surface of the skin. These are the muscles that are responsible for most of the movement of the torso, trunk, and neck. The deep muscles are much smaller and contribute very little to the larger phasic movements of the spine. However, they are rich in nerve endings, which relay messages to the brain, or *afferent* messages. These messages help coordinate the movement of these larger muscles. If smaller deep muscles are not toned, faulty messages may be relayed to the brain. As a result, faulty signals will be sent from the brain to the larger muscles in the spine causing segmental dysfunction, muscle spasms, poor flexibility, and pain.

Smaller, deep spinal muscles are exercised most when we are required to use our sense of balance. The human race was created to walk barefoot on dirt, sand, hills, beaches, etc. We should be stepping over rocks, running through muddy creek beds, etc. Instead, we walk on sidewalks and marble floors with an inch of shoe between the ground and us. As a result, these deep spinal muscles don't get the sensory input they need and they lose their tone, making your body susceptible to injury.

What are the three biggest benefits to be gained from chiropractic care?

1. **Prevention**: The first and foremost advantage of consistent chiropractic care is prevention. Imagine living your life completely free of aches and pains. Visualize yourself waking up every morning knowing that you are in top form and that your body is functioning at its maximum potential. Seeking chiropractic care now will ensure that you don't have to worry about costly and painful surgeries later on in life. You won't need that second or third hip replacement because you have been consistently taking care of your structure. Don't put yourself in a position where surgery becomes necessary, as with routine care it can be avoided altogether. **Consider this**: if

you spend $400 on a pair of tires but their alignment is off, they will never make it to the 50,000-mile mark. At most, they will make it to 30,000 miles. Your body is no different in terms of endurance. If you take good care of it, it will make it to the hundred-year mark like it's supposed to. If your joints are misaligned, bone buildup and joint swelling won't allow you to make it as far.

2. **Speeds up rate of recovery**: It's a proven fact that when you are injured, seeking chiropractic treatment significantly speeds up recovery. Trainers and coaches understand that daily adjustments are necessary for professional athletes to remain in top form. When he was in action, superstar Emmitt Smith made sure that he was adjusted before and after every game. I treat many professional athletes who simply cannot gamble with their million dollar sports bodies and need to be in prime form. These professionals do not only seek treatment for injuries but also undergo routine joint maintenance to make sure that they are not putting themselves at risk for developing any unnecessary injuries.

The average person does not have to see a chiropractor on a daily basis, but routine checkups are strongly recommended in order to catch something before it develops into a more serious condition. If there problems are detected, corrective care can make sure that they do not worsen. Once degeneration reaches a certain level, the most a chiropractor can do is provide pain relief rather than focus on corrective treatment. When you go through care, the frequency of your visits will depend on your condition and the recommendations of your chiropractor. The sooner you seek treatment, the sooner you can get back to living a pain-free life.

"I have always been a proponent of chiropractic care. The problem doesn't get fixed until I go to a doctor of chiropractic."

— Derek Parra, 2002 Olympic Gold Medalist and World Record Holder, Men's 1500 Meters

3. **Long-term savings**: Seeking chiropractic treatment a few times a year is much more cost effective than spending thousands of

dollars on back surgery in a decade. Evidence suggests that very few back surgeries are worth their cost, which can be anywhere from $20,000 to $100,000. Before investing in anything, you need to do a cost-benefit analysis. Very few households across America don't have cable TV, yet millions of people forgo chiropractic care, though they cost a similar amount. Ask yourself if living in constant pain or running the risk of joint damage in your future is worth saving a couple hundred bucks a year. Everyone can afford chiropractic care by looking at their household expenses very carefully and cutting out some frills. If cutting down your latte habit to four times a week is what it takes, it's well worth the sacrifice.

There seem to be a lot of myths about chiropractic care. What is the truth?

Myth #1

If you go to the chiropractor once, you always have to go.

Many people believe that if they go to the chiropractor once they are locked in for life. This is only half true. In reality, the frequency of your visits depends entirely on your desire to lead a lifestyle centered on wellness. For most people, going to the chiropractor should be like going to the dentist. Proper care between visits keeps your dental costs down, and the same can be said for chiropractic care. Proper stretching and strengthening on a daily basis, such as correctional exercise, Pilates, tai chi and basic stretches, will keep the fluidity in your joints that in turn will stop or slow down degenerative aspects of aging. You need only go a few times a year to ensure that there are no serious problems. Unless you have sports related injuries, perform repetitive non-ergonomic work such as repetitive bending or stooping, or have poor posture (all of which eventually lead to osteoarthritis), daily or weekly treatments wouldn't be necessary.

If you neglect your chiropractic health, you are setting yourself up for serious problems such as joint decay, aka degenerative joint disease (DJD). If joint decay goes undetected over an extended period of time, it can result in many pathological conditions such as disc herniations, disc bulges, osteoarthritis, and stenosis, which can lead eventually to costly back surgery.

Myth #2

You're getting your back cracked.

Contrary to popular belief, chiropractic does not center around simply "getting your back cracked." When a chiropractor works on you, he or she is treating any **subluxation** (when one or more bones in your spine move out of place and cause pressure on your spinal nerves) or bone misalignment you may have. Chiropractors are trained to look for misaligned joints and restricted tissue. When a subluxation occurs, a chiropractor corrects the misaligned/immobile segment and allows it to return to its proper position and movement. The correct term for this procedure is an **adjustment**, which is carried out with a quick thrust applied to a vertebra that allows the body to begin the healing process.

There are many ways this procedure can be performed and chiropractors use multiple techniques to achieve corrections to the spine. Ask your chiropractor for further details on his or her current techniques and what is best suited to treat your condition. The sound that so many patients refer to as a crack is actually the audible release of gas from the joints. The sound may be alarming to some patients, but it is also accompanied by relief. Think of it this way: when you were born, you had no restrictions to your spine or joints. Once life began, you started to have bad posture, stress, and poor ergonomics that caused your joints to become fixated or subluxated. This is why chiropractic care is so vital to wellness. Some patients may experience minor discomfort, but this is typically due to significant muscle tightness or simply because they were in a guarded state and too tense during the adjustment.

Myth #3

Chiropractors are not real doctors.

This is a myth. A chiropractor is a doctor of chiropractics. The truth is chiropractors and medical doctors complete the exact same curriculum up until their third or fourth year of study. Chiropractors actually clock more hours of classroom education than medical doctors do. What many people fail to understand is that the difference between a chiropractor and a medical doctor is not their level of education but the specific manner in which they choose to care for patients. Medical doctors, through their specialized knowledge of pharmacology, can focus on and treat diseases related to the organs through the use of medicine.

Chiropractors do not treat patients with medicine, nor do they have specialized knowledge in that field. Instead, chiropractors use physical solutions such as adjustments, exercises, stretches, and muscle therapy to address physical problems such as pain, muscle spasms, headaches, and poor posture. Just as if you were having a heart related disorder you would see the cardiologist who is the specialist for the heart, you should see the chiropractor for any and all musculoskeletal conditions related to muscles and joints.

For instance, a general practitioner knows the basics like the chiropractor but both refer to the cardiologist for expert advice on the heart. These should be the guidelines to which all doctors subscribe, but unfortunately many treat outside their true scope of practice. The guidelines that a chiropractor must follow are no different from those of a medical doctor. In both cases, the same structure of testing, licensing, and monitoring by state and national peer review boards is followed. Federal and state programs, such as Medicare, Medicaid, and workers' compensation programs cover chiropractic care, and all federal agencies accept sick leave certificates signed by doctors of chiropractic.

Myth #4

Chiropractors treat only neck, back, and spinal pain.

Chiropractors do not only treat neck, back, and spinal pain. They also can treat pain in the ankles, wrists, and all other joints. Chiropractic, in general terms, focuses on making sure that the structure and function of the body are in harmony. A majority of the problems experienced by patients stem from spinal misalignments that manifest themselves in other parts of the body. As a biomechanical specialist, I focus on the kinetic chain and the movement patterns of the entire structure and treat all joints, not just the spine.

One of the fundamental ideas of chiropractic treatment is that spinal nerves are negatively affected as they exit the spinal column, which in turn leaves a reduced motion to the segment and thus pain and swelling occur. These spinal nerves travel out to every structure in the body. If they are negatively affected they will be sending faulty signals and problems can arise. It is for this reason that spinal manipulation is so important to the overall health of the whole body, not just the neck and back as many think.

Success in Your Spine

Posture

Many people believe that having good posture simply means standing up or sitting up straight. While this is important, posture also has a tremendous impact on your overall health. In order to achieve good posture, your body needs to be properly aligned. Proper alignment is a condition in which your bones, rather than your muscles, support your weight. This results in a reduction in effort and strain on your overall structure. You can tell if your posture is misaligned if you feel aches or pains while going about your daily activities.

For instance, if you are walking and feel a pain in your right hip, this is due to abnormal movement. Having poor posture greatly interferes with everyday activities by distorting the alignment of bones, causing chronic muscle tension, and contributing to stressful conditions such as loss of vital lung capacity and increased fatigue.

Posture can be corrected in two primary ways: the elimination of bad stress and the application of good stress. Bad stress is caused by a variety of conditions such as a heavy purse or poorly adjusted car seat. Good stress utilizes a variety of exercises, adjustments, and stretches to move your body back to its natural state and restoring balance. Once proper posture is restored, you will have more energy and be able to move gracefully without any pain.

Movement

Proper, pain-free movement should never be taken for granted. Without the ability to move properly, every aspect of your life is greatly impacted. Even simple activities such as brushing your teeth and driving a car can suddenly become impossible. As a healthy body moves, it creates a negative pressure inside the disc space creating a natural pumping of fluid into your spine and hydrating disc spaces. Improper movement doesn't allow fluid to pump into all of those spaces, resulting in degenerative disc disease or disc dehydration. This will eventually require surgery if left undiagnosed. Proper care at this point is essential.

When the joints in one area of your body do not move properly, other areas are forced to work harder to compensate for the loss. This places a significant amount of stress on those joints and results in pain and inflammation. The areas without normal movement will slowly deteriorate as the muscles continue to tighten, joints stick together, and ligaments and tendons shorten. Chiropractic adjustments as well as exercise can help restore the body's natural movement, and help ensure that you enjoy proper, pain-free movement.

Strength

Strong muscles are essential to proper posture, movement, and balance. In order for your body to stand up straight and be strong, muscles on all sides of your spine need to be balanced. Weak, imbalanced muscles are common in many people due to lack of exercise and spinal misalignment. When your body is injured, you not only need treatment but you also need strengthening exercises afterwards. For instance, if your arm is in a cast for six weeks, it will heal, but it will be much weaker than your non-injured arm. In order to regain muscular strength in that arm you need strength training. Strength training allows you to get proper function back in a particular area and hold any adjustments that have been made. Many patients go to a chiropractor after an injury, but never heal because they simply do not engage in strength training exercises. Having strong muscles contributes to a pain-free lifestyle centered on wellness.

Balance

Balance is the maintenance of your center of gravity over your base of support, in both a static and dynamic posture(s), and in stable and ever-changing environments.

Your postural muscles are responsible for holding your body erect. Chiropractic adjustments are only as effective as the strength of your core muscles. Many injuries are caused when you move from a phasic movement, such as weeding, to a basic movement, such as standing up. A weak core cannot handle such a dramatic change in pattern, and this can result in injury. This is how you injure your spine. I hear it all the time: "Doctor, I was just bending over to pick up my socks from the floor," or "I was just bending over to put my shoes on and my back went out." This is why we ask every patient about their exercises, such as walking, swimming, tai chi, Pilates, bicycling, martial arts, and bodybuilding. All of these exercises help to improve muscle coordination and strengthen your core. Correct balance decreases your chance of injury as well as decreasing muscle aches and joint pain.

Chapter 4

Eat Well-Diet and Nutrition

"I've been going to chiropractors for as long as I can remember. It's as important to my training as practicing my swing."

—Tiger Woods, Professional Golfer

Nutrition Philosophy

YOUR BODY IS NOT meant to be overloaded with sugary, over-processed foods with no real nutritional value. Instead, it is meant to consume natural, raw foods that have not been denatured by overcooking. The ideal diet is composed of no less than 60% raw foods such as fresh, organic fruits and vegetables. This diet will pave the way for a more energetic body as well as heightened mental capacity. Our "Super-Size" culture has led many to believe that bigger is better and that less is not more.

Sadly, this philosophy has created a very unhealthy generation of youth. Studies reveal that today's children and adolescents are the first generation that is not expected to outlive their parents' life expectancy. According to the American Academy of Pediatrics, the American childhood obesity rate has doubled during the past two decades and tripled for teenagers. This early onset obesity will inevitably translate into lifelong obesity as well as serious chronic illnesses. This surge in obesity is a direct result of an unhealthy, over-processed diet. Look at sugary soda: it destroys the pancreas and floods the body with a dosage of unnatural sugars. Your body doesn't know how to utilize these sugars and reacts by becoming ill.

Your body has had enough of unnatural sugars and over-processed foods. I challenge you to actually try a natural, whole food diet for one month and you will see major changes in just this short time. I had a patient come into my office with type 2 diabetes. We put him on a 100% raw food diet with all the right supplements and enzymes. After eight weeks, he no longer needed his insulin shots; the diet completely reversed his diabetes. The diet essentially cleaned out his disease. That is just how powerful natural foods can be.

Why is the quality of what I take into my body so important to my health?

When it comes to what you put inside your body, quality is everything. Food can be divided into two main categories: natural and unnatural. Natural foods are always of a higher quality than unnatural foods. For instance, a banana is a living organism with enzymes that aid in the breakdown of its structure, while a hamburger from a fast food joint has no such enzymes. To put this to the test, grab a banana and a hamburger from your local fast food joint. Let the two items sit on your kitchen counter for a few weeks. Over time, you will see the banana break down and cannibalize itself. The hamburger will remain in the same condition as it was on day one. While it will shrink due to dehydration, there will be no decomposition. The hamburger has so many preservatives that it cannot break down.

This is prime example of a truly unhealthy, poor quality food versus one that is of high quality. Once you put the banana into your system it will start to digest itself and your body will get rid of it naturally. Alternatively, if you eat fast food it will take much longer for your body to get rid of it, if ever. Ever wonder why colon cancer is on the rise? Just think of all the crap (no pun intended) sitting in your GI tract right now. All these preservatives have to do is cause dysplasia which is the premalignant transformation and abnormal growth of cells on the surface of tissue, and that will typically lead to cancer.

Through an unhealthy diet, your GI tract is exposed to hormones that are unnatural and alien thus making it more susceptible to diseases such as colitis, Crohn's, and cancer. Patients who start a raw food diet often lose three to four pounds right away because of the waste that is eliminated from their colons. It's absolutely disgusting to think that a burger you ate last year is still in your body. Just imagine all of that extra weight you are carrying around and the countless opportunities for that waste to mutate into disease.

When you eat a fast food hamburger, you are not eating quality meat but rather meat that has been pumped full of growth hormones then shipped off to a lab and crammed with preservatives. If you go to a good quality steakhouse, you can immediately taste the difference. The meat tastes like meat, you don't have to bathe it in ketchup. Grass-fed, natural beef is much healthier and boasts a much higher quality than any burger you can buy for a buck. Turn to nature as an example. You don't see wild animals with heart problems, high cholesterol, or cancer, because they eat natural foods and have a natural diet. There are no fast food restaurants in the animal kingdom; every meal is caught and eaten fresh.

Quality also should not be compromised when choosing fruits and vegetables. In the past, farms used to harvest crops and leave the land barren for a few years in order for the soil to recoup its natural minerals. Nowadays, corporate farms focused solely on profit rather than providing quality goods take no such precautions.

Organic fruits and vegetables are of a superior quality because they have been harvested from natural minerals rather than synthetic ones. There is a vast difference between natural and synthetic minerals. If you ever have the chance to observe natural vitamin C under a microscope, you will see that is absolutely beautiful. It looks like a crystalline rainbow, something that is found in nature. On the other hand, synthetic vitamin C is structured and appears completely unnatural.

What are the main rules one must follow to supplement properly?

You need to supplement your diet by taking enzymes, probiotics, mineral supplements, and fish oil supplements on a daily basis. The more I study nutrition, the more I am convinced that we need to eat raw, uncooked, unprocessed food.

Cooked foods contribute to chronic illness, because their enzyme content is damaged and thus they require us to make our own enzymes to process the food. The digestion of cooked food uses valuable metabolic enzymes. Digestion of cooked food demands much more energy than the digestion of raw food. In general, raw food is so much more easily digested because it has all those natural enzymes that it passes through the digestive tract in half the time it takes for cooked food. I recommend the book *Fast Food Nation* by Eric Schlosser to truly understand what is going on in American culture with respect to the foods we eat.

Eating enzyme-dead foods places a burden on your pancreas and other organs and overworks them, which eventually exhausts these organs. Many people gradually impair their pancreas and progressively lose the ability to digest their food after a lifetime of ingesting processed foods.

1. **Enzymes** are critical because they aid in the breakdown of cooked and processed foods. They help remove these foods from

your system faster so there is less chance of any cell mutation. I recommend Standard Process Multizyme and "Flow" by ONEBODE.

2. **Fish oils** are essential because they contain **omega-3 fatty acids**. These acids soften the fats and plaque that build up in your arties and in doing so reduce the chance of heart related illness. Since people do not get enough good fats in their diets, it is important to supplement the body with these. It is also important to note that plant based sources of oil (nuts and seeds) are good sources as they are less likely to have toxic metals. These also do not cause the same level of acidity in the body as animal omega-3 sources.

3. **Mineral Supplements** help fill in any nutritional deficiency that you may have in your diet. It is important to remember that quality mineral supplements are key factors. Look for pills that have not been denatured and compacted with harsh chemicals but have been bonded with natural ingredients and have a "cGMP" certified stamp on the bottle.

4. **Probiotics**, as defined by the World Health Organization and Food and Drug Agriculture Organization of the United Nations, are "live microorganisms, which, when administered in adequate amounts, confer a health benefit on the host." This "good bacteria" can be found in yogurt as well as added artificially to other foods and supplements. Probiotics provide your intestine with a dose of good bacteria to promote a healthy gut.

When you shop for supplements, do your research and be sure to go natural, meaning whole food based. Look for products that are either GMP (Good Manufacturing Practices) certified or cGMP (Current Good Manufacturing Practices) certified. You know these are quality goods because their development has been tested by the Food and Drug Administration to ensure that all possible negative effects have been addressed. These products go through rigorous internal and external testing to ensure safety. It is not worth your time or money to bother with noncertified supplements. Many of these products have no value because of the way they have been prepared. Once an enzyme or supplement is denatured, it no longer has any value and can actually cause harm. For example, mineral supplements that are bonded to harsh chemicals have a harder time breaking down in your GI tract, which can result in disease. Don't be afraid to spend money on good supplements; as previously discussed, quality is everything.

A daily example of a perfect diet

It is ideal to eat six small meals a day, rather than infrequent large meals. Eating smaller meals doesn't overwhelm your body with large amounts of food, and allows it time to properly digest and remove waste. Blood sugar levels are also stabilized, ensuring that you have enough energy to get through the day.

Breakfast is the most important meal because it ensures your body has the right fuel to prepare it for the day. Ideally, breakfast should consist of raw fruits and freshly squeezed fruit juices. There is nothing wrong with eating pancakes or bagels but you need to make sure you take enzymes with these foods. Make sure you take all the essential supplements as discussed above. There are no excuses for skipping breakfast; it is the easiest meal of the day to prepare.

Snack on whole foods throughout the day, such as fresh fruits and vegetables. When eating out it is critical to watch your portion size. Do not eat everything that is put in front of you. Instead, try eating only 50% and wait for 20 minutes. Give your body enough time to tell your brain that it's full. If you don't want to throw away good food, there is no shame in asking for a takeout container. It is impossible to eat perfectly when dining out, but you can control how much you eat and opt for healthier choices such as lean rather than fatty meats.

Foods such as fruits, vegetables, free-range foods, and proteins should also be a part of every well balanced diet. When cooking at home, learn how to make your own salad dressings and condiments. This small effort is not only healthier but also saves you from the vast number of hidden calories in processed food. When shopping, it is best to go organic, which isn't as expensive as you may think. Even Costco carries organic chicken and milk. Learn how to put together good food combinations. Don't prepare meals that are full of meat and potatoes, and always remember that raw is better.

Your body is your most valuable asset and should not be neglected. Some people spend vast amounts of money on material possessions, but fill their bodies with dangerous chemicals and unhealthy foods. This is a complete contradiction. If you care about what is on the outside, you should care twice as much about what is in the inside. Instead of following the herd and not caring about what you eat, be proactive and do your own research or consult a nutritionist. In the long run, your body will thank you for it.

What is the best food diet to follow?

I believe the raw food diet is the best one that is out there currently and doesn't always have to be followed in its entirety, meaning a little of a raw food diet goes a long way in one's overall health. If you can live by 75% of your diet being raw you are headed in the right direction. A raw food diet is based on unprocessed and uncooked plant foods, such as fresh fruits and vegetables, sprouts, seeds, nuts, grains, beans, nuts, dried fruit, and seaweed.

Heating foods above 116° F destroys enzymes in food that can assist in the digestion and absorption of food.

What are the benefits of the raw food diet?

A raw food diet has numerous health benefits:

- Increased energy
- Improved skin appearance
- Better digestion
- Weight loss
- Reduced risk of heart disease

A raw food diet contains fewer trans fats and less saturated fat than the typical western diet. It is also low in sodium and high in potassium, magnesium, folate, fiber and phytochemicals—health promoting plant chemicals.

A raw diet is associated with a reduced risk of diseases such as heart disease, diabetes, and cancer.

The *Journal of Nutrition* found that consumption of a raw food diet lowered total cholesterol and triglyceride concentrations.

What are the guidelines of the raw food diet?

1. What can I eat?

Unprocessed, preferably organic, whole foods such as:

- Fresh fruits and vegetables
- Nuts
- Seeds
- Beans
- Grains
- Legumes
- Dried fruit
- Seaweed
- Unprocessed organic or natural foods
- Freshly juiced fruit and vegetables
- Purified water
- Young coconut milk

2. What cooking techniques are used?

Specific cooking techniques make foods more digestible and add variety to the diet, including:

- Sprouting seeds, grains, and beans
- Juicing fruit and vegetables
- Soaking nuts and dried fruit
- Blending
- Dehydrating food

3. What equipment can I use?

- A dehydrator, which blows air through food at a temperature of less than 116° F
- A good quality juice extractor for juicing fruit and vegetables
- A blender, food processor, or chopper to save time
- Large glass containers to soak and sprout seeds, grains, and beans
- Mason jars for storing sprouts and other food

Side Effects

Some people experience a detoxification reaction when they start the raw food diet, especially if their previous diet was rich in meat, sugar, white flour, and caffeine. Mild headaches, nausea, and cravings can occur but usually last only several days.

Precautions

The raw food diet may not be appropriate for certain people, such as:

- Children
- Pregnant or nursing women
- People with anemia
- People at risk for osteoporosis: A Washington University study found that people following a raw food diet had lower bone mass. Bone turnover rates, however, were similar to the group that ate a standard American diet.

Considerable time, energy, and commitment are needed to be healthy on the raw food diet. Many of the foods are made from scratch. Some ingredients may be hard to find, such as Rejuvelac (the fermented liquid drained from sprouted grains), sprouted flour, date sugar, young coconut milk, carob powder, and Celtic sea salt.

Chapter 5

Exercise

"Think health, eat sparingly, exercise regularly, walk a lot, and think positively about yourself."

—Norman Vincent Peale

Exercise

It is no secret that people who combine exercise with diet will lose more fat than those who choose diet or exercise alone. This is because the only way to eliminate fat is to use it as fuel for your muscles. On a diet alone you will lose weight, but what you lose is not necessarily fat. You may lose fat, water weight, muscle, and bone weight. Any program that allows you to lose muscle is counterproductive since muscle is the only organ that uses fat for fuel. A proper program will use the muscle tissue you already have more often; while increasing muscle mass for a continuous period of time and decreasing the intake of sugar and high glycemic starches (these can prevent fat from being used by your muscles), thereby improving body composition. This is the only way to ensure long-term fat loss.

Exercise has been proven to have many physical and metabolic benefits. When you exercise, you slow aging, even reversing some parts of the aging process. You maintain, and even gain, bone and muscle weight.

Regular physical activity will increase your metabolic rate even while you rest. This will increase the number of calories needed to fuel your body during and after exercise. Therefore, your body will burn more fuel, including its stores of fat. The thermic effect of food will increase as more of the new calories you intake will be used for heat rather than converted to fat. This is especially true for calories consumed after exercise.

After exercising, lipogenic enzymes that create fat will slow down. However, high glycemic sugars and starches, as well as fructose sweeteners, will increase the lipogenic process faster than exercise can slow it down. On the other hand, physical activity increases the activity of glycogen synthase; more blood sugar is used as glycogen (fuel) in muscle tissue. Therefore, lost blood sugar will be deposited as fat.

"Succes is a journey, not a destination."

— Ben Sweetland

While adipose tissue LPL is proficient at turning carbohydrates into fat cells, skeletal muscle LPL is not effective at using fat. Regular activity helps to reverse this process by encouraging the metabolically-active tissues (muscle and organs) to burn fat cells.

Once fat is stored in fat cells, it has a difficult time breaking away. Diets that are caloric restrictive, low carbohydrate, or low fat, can make this even worse. Exercise kick starts the elimination of fat and can even reverse the damage done by these diets. Activity will also make fat cells more responsive to the two catecholamine hormones (noradrenalin and adrenaline) that encourage fat burning. Exercise also increases the activity of hormone sensitive lipase, making it easier for fat to escape from the fat cells.

It's no secret that exercise benefits men and women differently. For fat cells in the upper torso, exercise is equivalent for men and women, but there are differences in the lower body. For men, beta receptors are activated more frequently and aggressively, which helps send the signals for fat to break away, while there is really no similar effect in women.

For women, exercise simply decreases the activity of the alpha-2 receptors that would normally prevent fat from breaking away. This is why it is more difficult for women to lose fat in the hips and thighs. Women must also address and their adrenal and sex hormone makeup. These factors affect the gain and loss of adipose tissue and fat. Women should get hormone levels checked after 40 or as early as 35 to so see if their adrenal hormones and sex hormones are balanced. These hormones include: cortisol, DHEA, estrogen, and progesterone. Women should also be sure to get their saliva and urine tested as well as blood. Conventional doctors usually only test blood. This method is great if your levels are way off, but in order for a hormone imbalance to show up in your blood, the level must be extremely low, and in my experience one person's levels are never the same as the next. One may function at a certain level just fine while another needs a higher level of (for instance) progesterone to keep her cognitive ability or libido in line or her weight loss in check for exercise. It is imperative that your doctor understands this relationship and that he or she doesn't test blood only. If this is all your doctor recommends, I would suggest seeking alternate counsel because he or she obviously doesn't understand this relationship.

Once fat has broken away, it must be used by active muscle tissue, otherwise it will return to fat cells. More muscle means more opportunities to burn fat. Exercise will increase enzymes that allow fat to enter the muscle tissue, and once there it allows the muscle to better utilize the fat. As this metabolic process continues, your body will continue to use fat stores for fuel.

While insulin may be the hormone that triggers the storage of fat, exercise helps to slow fat storage. During and after exercise, blood sugar and insulin levels are lower. Metabolically active muscle tissue will also make better use of the insulin. So, if you are planning the occasional dietary lapse, exercising beforehand will make it less damaging.

Exercise/Move Well

What is meant by moving well?

As the age old saying goes, "move it or lose it." In order to live a rich, long life free from aches and pains you must **engage in regular physical activity**. Exercise has been proven to have many physical and metabolic benefits, such as slowing the aging process as well as maintaining and gaining bone, muscle, and weight. In addition to ensuring your body stays in top form, regular physical activity also promotes fat loss faster than diet alone.

The only way to eliminate fat is to use the fuel in your muscles through physical activity. You will lose weight on a diet alone, but it is not all fat; rather, it is a combination of fat, water weight, muscle, and bone weight. Any program that allows you to lose muscle is counterproductive, since muscle is the only organ that uses fat for fuel. A proper program will use the muscle tissue you already have while increasing muscle mass for a continuous period of time as well as decreasing the sugar intake and consumption of high-glycemic starches (they can prevent fat from being used by your muscles). This is the only way to ensure long-term fat loss.

For children, exercise is an important part of neurological and emotional development. It allows their bodies to develop and form correctly. Regardless of age, exercise should be a part of your daily routine.

What are the basic stretches that I must do on a daily basis and why is daily stretching so critical to a healthy lifestyle?

The reason cats are rumored to have nine lives is because they are constantly stretching and moving, thus making themselves more resistant to injury. Stretching can be done in the form of Pilates, tai chi or corrective exercise. If you have the discipline to stretch on a daily basis, you can do it at home, by yourself, or with a DVD. Join a class if you need more discipline and accountability. Once you actually learn how to properly stretch and utilize these techniques, it will get easier to carry them out on a consistent basis so you can keep your body moving in a proper manner. The best time to stretch is in the morning when your body is waking up from an extended period of inactivity. These exercises can be performed in as little as 5-15 minutes, yet still yield effective results.

Everyone has two basic sets of muscles: the postural AKA "core" muscles and the phasic muscles. Postural muscles work involuntarily while phasic muscles are responsible for carrying out activities such as lifting objects. Both sets of muscles can be tuned with Pilates, yoga and regular exercise. When your postural muscles are tuned, you automatically will have a stronger phasic muscle, which will help you avoid injury.

What are the core components of a quality exercise plan?

Since exercise is so important for the health of your body and soul, daily physical activity is best. Exercising five days a week is also acceptable. You do not have to jog six miles, seven days a week; simply walking to the supermarket instead of driving is a form of exercise. You should stretch everyday and do at least 30-45 minutes of cardio, three to four times a week.

Exercise machines such as the Total Gym are designed to help you target all major muscles as well as focus on weight loss. The systems come fully equipped with all of the tools necessary for you to customize workouts. Just add a heart rate monitor to help you find your optimal heart rate. If you have any existing medical conditions, you must consult your doctor before beginning any exercise routine.

Functional training is what we emphasize in our office and if you look at the origins of functional training you will find it in almost all rehabilitation programs. Physical therapists and CCSPs (Certified Chiropractic Sports Physicians) have been developing exercises for decades that mimic what patients do at home, work, or sport in order to return them to their lives or jobs after an injury. Thus if a person's job required repetitive heavy lifting, rehabilitation would be targeted towards heavy lifting. So depending on your job or daily activities you should have a workout program tailored to your specific needs because no two people like the same activities. A functional trainer would teach weight bearing activities targeted at core muscles of the abdomen and lower back. Most fitness facilities have a variety of weight training machines, which target and isolate specific muscles. I tell patients to get into a gym or training facility to understand this foundational relationship between postural and physical muscle groups. The bottom line is that getting an exercise specialist to evaluate your needs is critical in all individuals to help them perform the activities of daily life more easily and without injuries.

What are the benefits of functional training or core stabilization?

Functional training will lead to better muscular balance and joint stability, possibly decreasing the number of injuries sustained during normal activity of or any sport. Core stabilization works by emphasizing the body's ability to move simultaneously through six degrees of motion. In comparison, while weight-training machines appear to be safer to use, they restrict movements to a single plane of motion, which is an unnatural form of movement for the body and may potentially lead to faulty biomechanical movement patterns. Standard resistance training machines are of limited use for functional/core training—their fixed patterns rarely mimic natural movements, and they focus the effort on a single muscle group, rather than engaging the stabilizers and peripheral muscles.

In 2009 Spennewyn conducted research, published in the *Journal of Strength and Conditioning Research*, which compared functional training to fixed variable training techniques.[3] This was considered the first research of its type comparing the two methods of strength training. Results of the study showed very substantial gains and benefits in the functional training group over fixed training equipment. Functional users had a 58% greater increase in strength over the fixed-form group. Their improvements in balance were 196% higher over fixed and they reported an overall decrease in joint pain of 30%. This is why it is so important to have a stabilization program.

Components of an effective functional exercise program

Specific to the individual: Any program must be specific; working environment, home, and sporting activities all have to come into play to give one a true specific core program.

Farraginous variety: It should include a variety of exercises in no fixed order that work on flexibility, core, strength, and balance. Some of those exercises should include:

- Cable machines
- Medicine balls
- Kettlebells

---

3   Spennewyn, K. 2008. Journal of Strength and Conditioning Research, January, Volume 22, Number 1

- Bodyweight training
- Physioballs (also called Swiss balls or exercise balls)
- Resistance tubes
- Rocker and wobble boards
- Whole Body Vibration equipment (also called WBV or Acceleration Training)
- Balance disks
- Sandbags
- Suspension systems

Progressive: Progressive training steadily increases the strength demand from workout to workout. While most people are aware of the need for this in relation to traditional strength training, it is sometimes overlooked in functional training. Functional training also means varying the speed of movement to make it more sport specific.

I suggest that you work with a therapist or trainer who specializes in the particular area and can custom design a program.

Chapter 6

Wellness for Kids

---

*"It's easy to make a buck. It's a lot tougher
to make a difference."*

—Tom Brokaw

Wellness for Kids

What is the biggest factor that leads to childhood disease?

Food additives are the number one cause of childhood disease in America. Many people believe that disease is a product of bad genes or bad luck, but this is simply untrue. Disease is a direct reflection of what you put inside your body. *The Blue Zones*, by Dan Buettner, investigates areas where people live longer, healthier lives and concludes that these people all follow a similar diet, rich with natural and raw foods. People in these areas have much lower rates of illness, such as cancer and diabetes, as well. This indicates that disease is not something that strikes by chance, or without warning. By consuming harmful foods, we not only destroy ourselves, but we also destroy our children. Ironically, in a society where technology and medicine are so advanced, we are regressing with regard to taking care of ourselves. By trading healthy, "slow" foods for convenience, we shorten our life spans and are taking our children down with us.

Invest in your children's future and health by providing them with natural and raw foods, rather than buying into the hype promoted by the Food and Drug Administration. The FDA is not primarily concerned about the health and well-being of your children, but functions on the basis of profit for corporations who pad their pocketbooks. Don't buy into the facade that the agency is a nonprofit government regulatory organization. The individuals who run the FDA are bought in the same way our politicians are.

Food companies openly try to convince the public that synthetic vitamins are just as effective as those based on whole foods. Take a look at any children's cereal box or snack food, and you will be bombarded with claims that the product is rich in vitamins and minerals. While the product may be rich in vitamins and minerals, these are created in a lab and have no real nutritional value. Though numerous recent studies have claimed that there is no difference between synthetic and natural vitamins, these have been widely disproven.

It is simply not true that eating healthier is more expensive and time-consuming. Eating healthier can actually be more economical both in the short- and long-term. Advance meal planning is necessary to take advantage of ripening produce and sale pricing on bulk items, such as organic beans or rice, but this preparation is definitely worth the effort for health benefits and food budgets. In addition, if you live in an area where you can grow a portion of your own produce, it's a great way to teach children about the wonders and benefits of healthful foods and can supplement your monthly food budget. Such everyday eating habits keep your child healthy and protected against disease, leading to lower medical bills and higher long-term savings.

Organic food cooperatives keep their prices low by forgoing fancy packing and labels, cutting out the middle man, and delivering fresh produce or organic grass fed meats (among many other treasures) to your area for convenience. They offer the freshest locally grown and seasonal food at equal to lower prices than the local supermarket. Plus, you can feel good knowing that you are helping put a few more coins in a family farmer's pocket. To find a food co-op or CSA near you, go to Localharvest.org, and ask around your local health food store or natural health practitioner if you don't find what you need online.

What is the importance of environment in my child's development?

While a healthy diet is fundamental, a positive environment for your child is equally important. **A positive environment is a place where your child can develop in a healthy, spiritual, and social manner.** A positive environment consists of three key elements: **attention, discipline, and security.** You can create a positive and nurturing environment for your child by investing your time and attention into him or her. Instead of coming home and turning on the television, come home and greet your family. Ask them how their day was, and really listen to what they have to say. Be sure to make eye contact with your children and ask them if they are having any struggles at school or in their personal lives.

If your children are little, scoop them up in your arms and make sure they know that you love them unconditionally, and enjoy the time you spend with them. Let them know that they are missed when you are away. Take an interest in their hobbies, and show them that you are truly interested in them, by remembering small details as well as important events in their day-to-day lives. It is easy to have a generic child/parent relationship, but one that is warm and genuine takes time to develop and constant nourishment to foster.

Along with the good times, there are inevitably going to be some challenging ones as well. Being a warm and attentive parent does not mean you can be a doormat. Children need discipline and to learn the difference between right and wrong. **Discipline can be defined as having a positive environment with guidelines.** When your children do something that is out of line, you need to step up and ensure that they avoid those same patterns in the future. You have to let them know that you are the parent and the authority figure, so the next time you tell your children to stop doing something, they will understand what you mean.

Children need security. They need to know that you are going to be there for them and that you are establishing limits for them. Children crave boundaries, so they know how far they can actually venture out without being harmed. They are not equipped to set their own rules or make their own boundaries, and should not be permitted to do so. You are the parent, and you are charged with their care. When you are loving and firm, you will gain their respect and your home will be a place of relative order and calm. (We are talking about kids, after all!)

What are the three most important elements I can implement to help lead my children to a healthy lifestyle?

1. **Nutrition**: If you teach your children healthy eating habits from a young age, chances are strong that they will carry out these habits throughout the course of their adult lives. There may be "seasons of resistance" where more patience is required on your part, as well as flexibility, but a good way to get around this resistance is to incorporate healthier versions of their favorite foods into the family's diet.

   Introduce new foods to children a few times, not just once. Allow them to choose some produce when you shop. Visit a farm and taste the produce freshly picked. Ask for their help in the kitchen. All of these things can create interest and teach that real food doesn't come from a can with a fancy label on it. Instill in children the importance of a natural, raw food based diet, rather than one that is filled with "yucky chemicals." Tell them how strong, smart, and healthy they will be. Emphasize how much faster they will be able to run, and how healthy foods make you feel good on the inside. If you are unsure of the importance of a mostly raw food diet, simply pick up a book or consult a qualified nutritionist. Trying is better than nothing. Start small and work your way into things slowly, without denying everything to them all at once.

2. **Practice what you preach**: Your children are a product of you and your actions. If you want to know what type of person you truly are, simply look at your children. You cannot tell your children not to smoke, drink, or do drugs if you do these things yourself. Children are very intuitive. Whether you realize it or

not, your children observe you and tend to adopt your habits, both good and bad. Think about what type of legacy you want to leave your children and what is best for them. Make them proud to be your children by leading your family by healthy example.

3. **Lead by example**: To teach your children the importance of family and respect, be sure to realize the value of what you have. Always take time out for your spouse and show that he or she is important. This will create a solid foundation for your children to learn from as well as ensure that your marriage stays strong long after your children leave home. In this era of rampant divorce, it seems easier to start over with someone else rather than stay and work things out. If you do stay, your children will not only have a healthier environment in which to grow up, they will also learn the value of a healthy marriage, and how to protect it.

4. **Exercise with your kids**: Have a healthy exercise program which you do daily. Your children will see that you are working on

keeping yourself fit and they will emulate this same attitude toward exercise if you do it and include them in your workouts. This will also give you quality time with them and many teaching moments can be achieved while working out. One is the power of focus or the power of goal setting, for example through timed miles.

Chapter 7

The Mindset for Vitality

"The way you think, the way you behave, the way you eat, can influence your life by 30-50 years."

—Deepak Chopra, MD

The Mindset for Vitality

Why are our thoughts so important?

YOUR WHOLE ATTITUDE TOWARD LIFE is determined by your thoughts. This is not some New Age phenomenon with no basis in reality, but a proven principle. Visualization is a powerful tool that has existed since the beginning of time, yet is only now gaining popularity in mainstream society.

When you think of something constantly, it starts to consume you, whether you realize it or not. Those thoughts seep into every aspect of your being and manifest themselves in various aspects of your life. They have a profound impact on your everyday actions, beliefs, and general outlook.

Some people choose to believe that thoughts and visualizations are not in the realm of reality and should be relied on as a last resort when things take a turn for the worse. Sadly, this type of attitude has a detrimental impact on your life. For instance, if you constantly focus on the negative aspect of a situation rather than the positive, everyday confrontations will become problems rather than opportunities. Winston Churchill once said, "A pessimist sees the difficulty in every opportunity; an optimist sees the opportunity in every difficulty." Life comes down to how you choose to view the world around you and whether you choose to believe that your glass is half full or half empty. Once you start realizing that the world is a place of infinite potential, you will be able to usher in more opportunity and more prosperity. As William Arthur Ward said, "The optimist lives on the peninsula of infinite possibilities; the pessimist is stranded on the island of perpetual indecision."

> ## *"Positive attitudes create a chain reaction of positive thoughts."*
>
> ## — **Unknown**

In order to truly achieve success in life, it is crucial to encourage others and turn a blind eye to the constant criticism that surrounds you. Remember that no matter how much good you do, there will always be critics. You cannot live your life by what others think or how your actions may look in their eyes. Many people make excuses and give up way too early because they are unable to handle criticism. Criticism is the only sure thing in our society, so always take it with a grain of salt. Learn to filter the constructive from destructive criticism and become your own biggest fan. Support your vision and your beliefs by feeding yourself encouraging thoughts on a consistent basis.

All of the greatest leaders throughout history have understood the importance of focusing on the positive. This is not merely a recent trend, but stretches as far back as the Bible: "Finally, brothers, whatever is true, whatever is noble, whatever is right, whatever is pure, whatever is lovely, whatever is admirable—if anything is excellent or praiseworthy—think about such things" (Philippians 4:8). Focusing on what is good in the world is an effective means of blocking out so much of the excess static, criticism, and negative thinking we see on a daily basis.

To find true joy, focus on what you can do for others rather than your own problems. Putting effort and energy into the prosperity and happiness of others will cut back on the amount of energy you put into your negative thoughts. You don't have to be Mother Teresa and abandon all of your earthly possessions, but you do need to put others first.

Positive thinking is the fountain of youth. According to the Mayo Clinic[4], those who think positively enjoy the following benefits:

- Increased life span
- Lower rates of depression
- Lower levels of distress
- Greater resistance to the common cold

4   (http://www.mayoclinic.com/health/positive-thinking/SR00009)

- Better psychological and physical well-being

- Reduced risk of death from cardiovascular disease

- Better coping skills during hardships and times of stress

It is a proven fact that your thoughts have a direct impact upon your health. Doctors have known for years that the fastest route to health is by avoiding stress and staying positive. A study of Coronary Heart Disease (CHD) in elderly men published in *The Journal of Biobehavioral Science*[5] found direct evidence that an optimistic attitude lowers the chances of developing CHD. The authors wrote, "[this] data are among the first to demonstrate that a more optimistic explanatory style, or viewing the glass as half full, lowers the risk of CHD in older men." The study explains that having a positive attitude enables you to cope with stressful situations more effectively, thus reducing the amount of stress placed on your body.

Further, the study claimed that "optimism may allow individuals to mobilize highly effective coping resources (psychological, social, and behavioral) when confronted with adversity. Thus, explanatory style affects an individual's ability to adapt to a myriad of environmental demands and seems to be stable across time and situations." With this concrete evidence that a positive attitude has a direct impact on your

---

5   (Kawachi et. al). (http://www.psychosomaticmedicine.org/cgi/content/full/63/6/910)

physical health, there are no excuses for remaining negative. Negativity kills.

Some people refuse to accept responsibly for their life. They harbor resentment against the world and continue to believe that they were shortchanged. You need to realize that your situation is a direct result of all your cumulative life decisions, beliefs, and actions. You made the choice to be in this situation. While it is true that some of us have had opportunities handed to us by the previous generation, ultimately we make the decision whether or not to embrace these opportunities. Your thoughts have created your present situation. If you continue to believe that there are no opportunities, you will never find any. This has been proven over and over again by poor immigrants who flee from their impoverished countries to become success stories in America. Even if you were dealt a bad card, you need to find a way to overcome your challenges and create a better life for yourself. If you continue to dwell on how awful your situation is, you will never improve.

Even in today's tough economy, people don't understand that America is the land of opportunity and there are still plenty of chances for success. Successful people have the right attitude and mindset; they put their best foot forward and embrace a healthy lifestyle. A balance in life is the answer. If you have past issues that are unresolved, seek out a wise counselor. Get started with the correct diet so you can remove the static and think more clearly. If you continue to put toxins in your body, you will create a breeding ground for disease. If you are riddled with disease, it will be much harder to continue to maintain a positive mindset and move forward.

Attitude

"Ability is what you're capable of doing.
Motivation determines what you do.
Attitude determines how well you do it."

—Lou Holtz

Attitude affects your vitality, overall health, and energy levels. Attitude is everything and everywhere. It precedes you even before you walk into a room. If you have a negative attitude, people can see it a mile away. They can feel your loathing and your self-pity. If you have a positive attitude, you can inspire people and make them feel good. You're never going to have good self-discipline or positive growth without the right attitude. Negative people do not become successful because they do not allow themselves to take on new challenges. Are you a boost for those around you? Are you the turbo engine in your workplace or home life? Bringing a positive attitude to those around you will be the boost to achieve greatness in their lives. Are you the wind beneath their wings or the anchor for their boat?

Everyone can train himself or herself to develop a more positive attitude by practicing these three keys:

1. **Positive self-talk**: Give yourself some credit and embrace your many gifts. Concentrate on what you can do rather than what you can't do. Once you start appreciating your positive qualities, a better self-image will follow.

"It's not what happens to you that determines how far you will go in life; it is how you handle what happens to you."

—**Zig Ziglar**

You will be challenged in many areas of your life. It is your reaction to these challenges that will help you achieve greatness.

2. **Surround yourself with positive people**: Avoid those who bring you down and add no benefit to your life. Be around positive people who have energy that

will lift you up rather than bringing you down. Positive thinking people are beneficial to all of us. They will affect how we act and how we deal with our surroundings. These individuals help us improve our own self-esteem and the way we feel about ourselves. I'm sure you can think of an individual about whom you say every time he or she enters the room, "wow, what a breath of fresh air." Their charismatic attitude is something you want to catch. I always ask my staff, "Is your attitude something anyone would want to catch today if it were a cold?" In stark contrast we can also think of that person who brightens up the room when they leave.

"Take charge of your attitude. Don't let someone else choose it for you."

—Anonymous

Thinking positively has many benefits. It gives you a clearer head and better memory, it makes it easier to make decisions and deal with situations, but above all it gives you a better and clearer outlook on life and makes you able to see the good out of the bad.

If you see half a glass of water, do you see it as half empty or half full? If you see it as half full, you are thinking positively. By thinking positively in all situations, which means having the right attitude in all situations, you will find that you broadcast joy to all those you come in contact with daily.

3. **Humor is the spice of life**: You cannot take life too seriously. We all make mistakes and do embarrassing things. The trick is learning how to brush the small things off and being able to laugh at yourself. The next time you do something silly, humor yourself rather than worrying about what other people are going to think. You can turn your stresses into fun with an attitude shift if you focus on maintaining a sense of humor in your daily life. With a lighthearted attitude, events that would normally be annoying become amusing, big hassles become humorously absurd,

major stressors become really great stories waiting to be told. Having a sense of humor is a big part of having fun— it's a way to actively seek out fun and happiness instead of waiting for it to come to you.

Chapter 8

Family and Relational Awareness

"To the world you may be one person, but to one person, you may be the world."

—Unknown

What is love?

LOVE IS TRULY CARING for another, without expecting anything in return. When you truly love someone, you do things for him or her without expecting any reward in return.

Why is love the most fundamental thing you need to be happy?

Without love, we are lost. Without love, we don't have that deep affection that we crave and need to be fulfilled. Regardless of where you are in life, you have the need to be loved and to give love to someone else. When I talk about love, I am not speaking specifically about romantic love. Not everyone wants to marry. I am talking about an unconditional love. Most people are at their best when they are doing things for those they love because they feel as if they are making a positive impact in the life of another person.

How does the need for love bring us into the subject of relationships?

Love, relationships, and attitude are all connected. As the quote goes, "I may not be able to change the world I see around me, but I can change what I see within me." Relationships are all about your attitude and the effort you are willing to put into them. If you have a bad attitude, you are not going to seek out the right relationships and you will never fully love or be loved in the way you truly need.

You attract people with like minds. When you love something, you are willing to serve, without regret. As JFK taught us, servitude is asking "not what your country can do for you, but what you can do for your country." He was speaking about servitude in the perfect form. He was able to motivate individuals to focus their energy onto each other and make us realize that life is putting our love into ideas. Servitude allows you to develop strong relationships that spill over into business and every other aspect of your life. For example, if you volunteer to help the needy, you won't get anything tangible in return, but will develop real relationships and be reminded that people are positively impacted by your contribution to their lives.

Why are relationships so important to our happiness?

There is no greater happiness than hearing a thank you from someone upon whose life you have made a positive impact. I have many different patients who tell me every day how grateful they are for what I've done for them. In all honesty, it never gets old. I never get tired of hearing how I made a positive difference because it makes me feel good and enriches my life. If for some reason I could no longer practice chiropractic, I would find another way to pay the bills, but I would continue practicing and helping people free of charge because of the joy it brings me.

Having a healthy and happy family life keeps me focused on serving others. Contrary to popular belief, money cannot buy happiness. Some of the richest people in the world are also the most miserable, because they have been unable to nurture healthy relationships. Servitude and thoughtfulness is what brings about true inner wellness, because when these components are in harmony, your body is more balanced.

Healthy relationships will also give you a richer life. Unhealthy relationships are negative and should be avoided at all costs. When you are constantly stressed, it is going to promote an unhealthy pH balance in your body thus bringing down your quality of life.

What are the three main elements to have ever growing and joyful family relationships?

1. **Make time**: It is so important to make time for family even when you are extremely busy. You have to spend quality time with your family in one form or another on a daily basis. You need to take a vacation, set aside one day of the

week strictly for family, and reflect on the relationships you have. For example, my wife and I take time out on a weekly or monthly basis to ask each other where we are in our relationship and how we can improve.

Your relationship with family is no different from a bank account; you cannot constantly withdraw without putting anything in. My schedule is very hectic, so I delegate. Even if you are extremely busy, you still need to figure out how to make time for family. If you work 70 hours a week, figure out how to work 60 and delegate the other 10 hours. When you're 90 years old and lying on your death bed, work will be the last thing on your mind.

2. **Add value**: Ask your family members how they feel about you and your relationship with them. Ask them what type of things they are struggling with at the moment and do your best to help them. For instance, at the moment my oldest son is learning how to express intense emotion appropriately. I am helping him control his temper more effectively. We try different techniques

and communicate on why he feels the way he does. The most important thing is that he knows he can confide in me when he is struggling. He knows that I care, and that I want to be a part of his life and raise him with character and integrity.

3. **Leadership in the home**: Be a leader in your home while being respectful to each member of the family. The father is the backbone of the family, while mothers are nurturing. Discipline is the responsibility of the father. In our society, we have so many families struggling and many men don't realize the importance of being a good father. All good fathers want the best for their children and want them to carry their legacy. Your children are a reflection of you and your character. After you're dead, your character will live on. Having a healthy and productive relationship with your family is important, yet is only one piece of the puzzle if you really want to have a true purpose. You can't have a healthy body if you focus on exercise and diet alone. Just because you are healthy doesn't mean you have a healthy home

life. You need to examine where you are going and how happy your family is with you and your home.

How important are relationships in your business and why?

Business is all about building healthy relationships. If people know that you are a person of integrity, they will refer others to your business. If you lack integrity, even your own friends will be afraid of referring you because they are afraid of what kind of business you run. If your friends don't trust you, why should anyone else? The stronger your relationships are with those who surround you, the stronger your business is going to be. One of the things that is key to your success as a small business owner is the ability to build relationships with other people. It's doubtful you'll be successful if you are socially inept and can't communicate your product or service. It's a fact that your success is dependent on you, it's that simple.

"Success has nothing to do with what you gain in life or accomplish for yourself. It's what you do for others."

— **Danny Thomas**

What is a step I can take today to strengthen the relationships within my business?

Be genuine. Be true to people, serve them, and want them to succeed. In order to strengthen your business relationships, put on the servitude hat and forget what you want from other people. There is no greater joy than serving others. True relationships can really bring about positive change. In a true relationship, people are honest with you and tell you things you may not want to hear, but they often know what is best for you. Get into someone else's shoes and find out where they are at and what they have to say. There is so much peripheral noise in our lives, but we need to realize that people just want to be heard.

Learn as much as you can about everyone you work with. Then, act on that knowledge. You need to know as much as possible about everyone, from your customers to your employees, so that when their needs change, you can be there to provide them with what they need to stay happy with your business, which is really you if it's a small business.

Treat your vendors like your best employees. It's important to nurture relationships with these individuals who aren't necessarily working for you but who service you regularly. This can mean anyone from the Staples delivery guy who stops by every week to the countless suppliers who keep your office stocked.

Know something special about everyone, like their favorite hobby or birthday. You might be thinking, "How much of a difference will saying 'Happy birthday' really make?" People love to be acknowledged and thought of, no matter the reason. And in a world where everyone is so wrapped up in their own agendas, getting a happy birthday wish from the people you regularly come into contact with is becoming a rarity. This shows caring and a spirit of true relationship building.

Encourage a sense of ownership among your employees. Whether it comes from having a say or input in major decisions, being able to inspire your employees to love your business as much as you do will strengthen your company's foundation and your business will be that much more likely to survive.

Great heights in business are only achieved when others follow and then lead when the lead dog has shown how to lead by example. You have to lead by example. I once had a small office and only a few staff. I would clean the bathroom myself two or three times daily. No one liked cleaning this bathroom because it was a very busy small office and the bathroom got used a lot so that it was filthy by the time lunch rolled around. I would clean it daily at lunch and then at the end of the day. Now when I got busier and simply could not find the time to do these things I had one of the staff do it, but she knew that if I asked her to do something that it wouldn't be something I wouldn't do myself. This example goes a long way because my staff knew that I didn't see myself as being above them or that I was the important doctor and they were the employees. They knew that we were a team and that I wouldn't ask them to do something that I wouldn't do or hadn't already done.

When you sell something, don't be mendacious. If it's something that you would buy and something you believe in, then sell it. You have to be true to yourself and when you're mendaciously bending the truth you cheapen the integrity of the sale and I can guarantee you that it will also be your last sale to that person and their circle of influence.

Have one-on-one conversations with your customers to find out what you can do better. Take or send out a survey. This will give you amazing insight into your business. People will not approach you with a detailed list of the things they'd like for you to improve on.

Constantly recognize a job well done. Employees love to be told they've done a good job on something. Most of the time, people who are interested in working for small businesses are driven more by recognition than by dollars. Never miss an opportunity to give your employees the recognition they deserve. And when a client compliments an employee's work be sure to pass the impressive review along to the staff person and be sure to point it out to everyone. It's good for their morale to know that recognition might be coming their way some time in the future.

Chapter 9

Living with Purpose

"What man actually needs is not a tensionless state but rather the striving and struggling for a worthwhile goal, a freely chosen task."

- Viktor Frankl, "Man's Search For Meaning."

Living with Purpose

What is purpose?

SINCE WE WERE TODDLERS, each of us has been hounded with the age old question, "What do you want to be when you grow up?" As children, we often have big dreams, and hope that we grow up to be someone great and vastly important. A lucky few are wise enough to realize their purpose in life at an early age, while it takes others a while longer to understand what they are meant to truly do. **I define the word *purpose* as my driving force in life and what is behind all of my actions, no matter how big or small.**

From a relatively early age, I realized that my life's purpose was to serve others and this fundamental force has provided direction and focus for the rest of my life. Without any type of focus, it is impossible to achieve any of the things you want out of life. Once you define your own purpose, it becomes much easier to steer your life in the correct direction.

Why is purpose important?

Imagine being aboard a beautiful yacht, but instead of stopping at exotic designations, you simply drift aimlessly. Sure, it might be entertaining for a while but eventually the thrill would wear thin. Without purpose, you are lost and will float from one thing to another. You will continue to search without any certainty as to what you are searching for. Without purpose, nothing in life brings true satisfaction. For example, in the modern workforce, millions of people get up in the morning, drag themselves to work, and do their jobs. They do just enough to get by so the boss will not replace them or so that they will qualify for the next bonus, but they do not really put their hearts into their work. As soon as the clock hits five they race to the nearest bar to have a drink and complain about how horrid their boss is or they go home and numb themselves with hours of pointless television.

Clearly, not having a purpose sets people up for a life of "just getting by" rather than one of passion, excitement, and dedication. Alternatively, those who do lead purposeful lives gain endless amounts of satisfaction. They don't watch the clock praying for the little hand to reach five, or surf the web to pass the time, but rather they put all their energy into the tasks at hand.

Without purpose, you cannot achieve your ultimate life goals. You won't ever have that solid foundation on which to build the other facets of your life. In my marriage, I often take the time to reflect on our foundation and remind myself why my wife and I got married in the first place. The same goes with every other area of my life. I always go back to the fundamental reason why I chose the particular path I did, and find that the answer always brings me back to my ultimate purpose in life, to serve others. True joy comes from knowing your purpose.

You can have more than one purpose, in the sense that you can have certain purposes in different "seasons" of life. However, you will have only one fundamental, overall, purpose that grounds all that you do. Ask yourself the question, why was I put on this earth? If you truly take time to reflect on this question, you will begin to better understand purpose in life. Were you a mistake? I don't believe so; you have a purpose which you were designed to fulfill.

"The meaning of life differs from man to man, from day to day and from hour to hour. What matters, therefore, is not the meaning of life in general but rather the specific meaning of a person's life at a given moment."

—Viktor Frankl, Man's Search for Meaning

Clarify your purpose

In order to clarify your purpose you need to reflect on what makes you joyful. The things in life which bring you joy are those which will lead you to your natural purpose. When things are prosperous regardless of what profession you are in, it is a sign that you are probably doing what you are meant to be doing. Even when times are difficult, having the right purpose will still bring you satisfaction despite the fact that you may not be making as much money. For most people, what gives them joy creates happiness and fulfillment in others as well. When others are grateful for your presence in their lives, you know that you have found your purpose.

Purpose cannot be a one-way street, but rather needs to bring happiness to yourself and those around you. For example, Michael Jackson was mourned by billions the world over because of the joy he brought to the world as an entertainer. By singing and dancing professionally, he fulfilled his own life's purpose, but also inspired and brought happiness to his fans. Of course, not everyone will reach billions of lives, and that's perfectly fine. Your purpose can be to be the best dentist you can possibly be so at the end of the day you know you have reduced your patients' pain and suffering by giving them the care and treatment they needed. You might also be a schoolteacher determined to make young lives better. The point is that your purpose and actions must have a positive impact, no matter how big or small. In the end, your purpose is empty if it is not shared with others. The world's happiest people are not necessarily the richest, but the ones who have found their purpose and brought joy to those around them.

Does purpose change as we move into different seasons of our lives?

Your general overall purpose can be defined very early on in life, and you should strive to discover what that is as soon as possible. The sooner you do, the sooner you will figure out other aspects of your life. Basically, in order to have your life in focus, you need to find your purpose first regardless of your age. I know my purpose in life is serving others. When I focus on serving others, everything else in my life falls into place. I was fortunate enough to find my purpose at an early age and this set the framework for all the other aspects of my life. When I was 16 years old, I decided to become a chiropractor because of a patient who had come out of my father's office in a state of pure joy and gratitude. She said that what happened felt like a religious experience to her because my father had eased her pain despite the fact that countless other doctors could not. Seeing her thank my father and seeing how grateful she was made me realize I wanted to bring the same kind of joy into people's lives. Giving people the freedom to move without pain brings them an immense amount of happiness and in turn gives me joy.

I do not believe your ultimate purpose changes over time. Your may have stepping stones and you can have more than one purpose, but there is a foundational purpose at your core. For example, my wife and I have purpose through our careers, but we also find purpose and satisfaction through philanthropy and charity, and through rearing our children. If you ever want to take the focus off yourself, just have a couple of kids!

People tend to get caught up in a negative cycle due to bad habits. Habits can be powerful or destructive and they shape you as a human being. When you have healthy habits, you are constantly going to attract prosperity and success, but unhealthy habits will ultimately lead to failure. Do unto others as you would like them to do unto you, because we all have someone who looks up to us, whether it is a patient, child, or spouse. If you don't have or know of anyone who is looking to you for direction, support, and advice, you might question whether or not you are moving in the right direction.

We need to be inspired to positive action by people around us, but we also need to inspire others to want to be their best as well. Once this behavior comes on a regular basis and without much effort, it is solid sign that you have discovered a truthful purpose. Anyone can make the changes needed to develop the correct attitude by acquiring the correct habits. For example, if you're trying to quit gambling, you have to examine the habits that keep you in that negative cycle. Do you spend all of your time playing poker online instead of other, more productive activities? Do you bet even if it is in a workplace pool? After you identity the habits, you can work on changing them and making positive progress in your life.

When you have a purpose...

When you have an ultimate purpose, life becomes an opportunity. I wake up excited to get to work and I rarely lose that excitement throughout the course of the day. When I leave the office to spend time with my family, I maintain that sense of excitement, because that, too, is something that is a part of my life purpose.

"Once an individual's search for a meaning is successful, it not only renders him happy but also gives him the capability to cope with suffering."

—Viktor Frankl, Man's Search for Meaning

Sometimes discouraging moments come that threaten to put a damper on an otherwise fruitful and productive day. When that happens, I go back to the core reasons I have chosen to be a doctor of chiropractic. I love helping people to heal, which paves the way for more success in their lives. It positively affects their families and personal lives, their self-esteem, their mental state, and it gives them the freedom to live their lives without limits.

I remind myself that I have no control over the choices that others may make, and their attitudes toward my staff or me. I remind myself that I am not responsible for what others may think of me or my decisions. It's my job to go to the office and focus my energy on my patients, and to inspire them to better health the best way I know how. Beyond that, it's really up to them to take that information and use it to better their health and life.

There are, unfortunately, always those who would rather not take responsibility for their own life decisions. Again, I try not to get discouraged by this, because I am only able to share information with these individuals, and my hope and prayer is that they will take what I have shared to heart and make a change for the better. I am bolstered by the fact that the sad stories are few and far between and the vast majority of the wonderful people I work with are willing to do what it takes to achieve the results they desire in their health and life.

Having a life full of purpose follows you no matter where you go. For example, there are times when I am grocery shopping and patients come up just to thank me for helping them. In my practice, I also do a lot of nutritional counseling and many people are completely changed as a result of a few nutritional tips or additions. The feeling of transforming a patient's life through education and treatment is the best way I feel I can serve humanity.

How can you tell whether someone is living with purpose?

Spotting someone who is living with purpose is easy. When someone is living a life full of purpose, you can see the joy in his or her life and the joy in the lives they impact. In short, a life full of purpose is a life full of joy. It's a life of living each day to the fullest, and not wasting opportunity when it presents itself. A person who isn't living a life full of purpose is usually miserable and directionless. The people around them are usually frustrated with them rather than joyful. A lot can be gathered about people simply by what their loved ones have to say about them. If you lack integrity in your business dealings, it will come back to you in one form or another. You may make a lot of money in the short term, but in the long-term you aren't doing something that is ultimately fulfilling and you're bound to get constant negative feedback, leading to eventual burnout and, probably, depression and maybe even a crisis at midlife.

If a real estate agent is continually selling "bad" houses at inflated prices, he or she won't get any referrals.

By contrast, a real estate agent who focuses on meeting the needs of his or her clients doesn't have to lie or engage in tricks. Such agents have the good sense to know that if they have patience and work hard for their clients, their businesses will steadily increase by word of mouth. Reputation isn't something that is built in a day, but it's something that reaps great rewards when it is maintained. Long-term success is based on focusing on the clients rather than viewing them as simply a sum of money. If you focus on what makes successful people successful, it's usually the purpose that drives their actions in all areas of their life. You have to add value to people in order to have true purpose. How do you add value to people?

People will validate it by what they say to you and what they write about you. People won't go along with you unless they can get along with you. You add value to others when you truly value them and the relationship. When you use them to step on or use them to your advantage, you do the complete opposite. Putting trust in someone before they trust or believe in you is how you get them to understand that you believe in them and by doing this you add value to them.

The greatest joy in life won't come from your own accomplishments. It will come from accomplishments by which you inspired greatness from someone else. When this happens you will be able to tell that you are living with true purpose.

Procrastination

"Procrastination is one of the most common and deadliest of diseases and its toll on success and happiness is heavy."

—Wayne Gretzky

Procrastination is the single most destructive thing that a person can engage in. Procrastination is the destroyer of dreams. If you don't have focus or drive to take action when necessary, then you're just going to sit back and let opportunity pass you by. You have to physically get up and do things rather than just talk about doing them, and take at least one positive action every day toward achieving your goals. If it hasn't happened yet, keep trying! Persistence is how the greatest inventions in history have been perfected. As Albert Einstein said, "I am not particularly intelligent, I just sit with a problem longer than most." If these creative, talented people had quit after their tenth attempt, we would not be where we are as a civilization.

Successful people are forged through discipline and the inner drive to achieve something great. In order to do something amazing, you have to believe in your gut that you can do it, and then take actions every day until you have achieved it. It is pointless to sit on the sidelines and complain. It takes work and diligence to accomplish great things.

Does purpose make you work with urgency?

When you have purpose, you have drive and urgency that motivates you to push through rough times. Having purpose gets you through rough times by helping you remember the foundation of your being. For instance, adults know that there is no such thing as perfection in marriage. The reality and stress of life can set in and steal the romance from the relationship if it is not carefully guarded. There are times when marriage can be challenging, but when that happens long-term damage can be avoided by remembering the fundamental reason you married your spouse. People evolve and change throughout life, but I often consider and reflect upon the specific reasons I fell in love with my wife and my purpose with her. It always brings me back to center and helps me realize the bigger picture of our life together. There are always challenges in life. It's the way you deal with them that counts.

I like to think of challenges in my life as opportunities for growth. We always have the choice of how to react to a given situation. We may not always be able to choose what happens, but we can choose our attitude toward events and how we will react. We can choose to react with clarity, keeping the big picture in mind; or we can react out of emotion, with little thought as to how our words and actions might affect others. I have been guilty of this shortsighted reaction many times, and it's something that I work on daily.

It's not worth doing emotional damage to people we love because of a simple lack of discipline on our part. We live in a society that is trained to give up too easily if things don't go our way. This is why we have one of the highest divorce rates in the world. Your lifelong purpose will allow you to get through tough times in your marriage and in your life because if you go back to basics, you remember your reasons for choosing your spouse or for pursuing your purpose in life. This kind of thinking will bring you back to what's truly worth fighting and living for. What really matters? If you're a salesperson and the economy is down, you can get through the rough times by focusing on what you can do for others rather than on your dwindling paycheck at the end of the month.

Purpose also allows you to overcome tragedies such as death and illness because it reminds you why you are still alive. The loss of a loved one is painful, and grieving must take place, but eventually things will get better. You can take comfort in the fact that your loved one would want you to continue on your life's path and impact the world in a positive manner. People who do not have a well-defined purpose usually take longer to recover from tragedy. Some never do. In order to make sure you can weather any storm that may come your way, you must define your purpose. It always comes back to having a fundamental purpose in life.

Chapter 10

Critical Factors for Success

*"Motivation is not a matter of will-power;
it is a matter of want-power."*

—Paul Karasik

Decide What Exactly You Want

"A goal without a plan is just a wish."

—Larry Elder

What are goals?

GOALS CAN BE DEFINED as the important benchmarks in life that you set for yourself. In order to be truly fruitful, they need to be measurable so you can gauge exactly how much progress you have made. Not setting goals is like wandering around in the dark without a flashlight. You will never be able to tell where you are going. If you don't set goals, you simply cannot reflect on how far you have come and what you have accomplished. You will not be able to effectively analyze what you have been doing correctly and what you need to improve upon. If you do not take the time to reflect on what is working and what is not, you will become stagnant and steer yourself further and further away from your dreams.

Goals can be either big or small depending on the area of life on which you are concentrating. Goals for family, your social life, and professional life all deserve equal attention. It is not enough to sit down once a year and make a New Year's resolution; you actually need to reflect on these goals on a regular basis. Write down your goals in order to make them more realistic and keep you on course.

For example, one of my personal goals is to learn how to speak Spanish. Instead of keeping this goal on the back burner and coming back to it when fancy strikes, I keep it alive by writing down Spanish phrases on flashcards and placing them in plain view. This forces me to practice my phrases and gives me a sense of accountability. So far, it has been paying off. When a Spanish-speaking patient steps through my door, I am able to communicate and treat him or her in basic Spanish. Of course, I still have a long way to go in terms of conversational Spanish, but I keep at it. I review those flashcards whenever I get a chance and practice speaking when the opportunity arises. Progress should be a lifelong goal regardless of the area on which you are concentrating. Progress is the foundation of life because without it, you are essentially dead.

Having clear goals also brings the gift of mental clarity. As soon as you know what you want, you will see so much of the excess static in your life disappear. Naturally, if you have no clear goals you will have no way of measuring your achievements and failures. Many things in life require clear vision, focus, and action. These pillars need to be aligned properly in order to achieve true success. With clarity, you can pinpoint if you are headed in the right direction in terms of achieving your goals, or if you are steering off course.

There are millions of people who do not realize how they got where they are because they never took the time to consider the decisions that led to their current circumstances. Remember that every choice you make has a direct impact on your circumstances. In order to make the right decisions, you need to have clarity and the only way clarity can be achieved is by setting goals.

Make Your Profession a Mission

Imagine living in a world where waking up each morning was an adventure rather than torture. For most people, the weekends are blissful time away from their dreary work weeks. Instead of feeling fulfilled or happy to have a job that they love, they feel trapped and utterly miserable for the better part of the week and live for a two-day break. Luckily, life doesn't have to be a mind-numbing rat race. We live in a country that is filled with countless opportunities, so there should be no excuse for staying in a job that makes you feel depressed or working at a place you feel isn't suited to your strengths.

There are certainly times in life where you are in a job, not a career, but I would prefer to think of those situations as temporary and immediately necessary rather than permanent.

We should all find a profession that infuses us with passion and inspires us to grow and be our best every day. **Professional passion can be defined as enjoying what you do to a point where it no longer feels like work but becomes something to enjoy.** Without any passion for your work, you will never be able to serve others effectively or stretch yourself beyond your comfort zone. You will only be able to do a mediocre job, and as a result you will become even more stressed over your lack of progress. This emotional distress will manifest in a physical manner in the form of joint pain, headaches, and other illnesses.

Success never comes easily, but if you have passion, it will make the struggle all the more worthwhile. Striving to be at the best in your profession comes from a natural desire to perform well and to serve others. The most successful athletes in the world do not stop training once they reach the top. They continue to train even harder to remain there.

Once Michael Jordan became a legend, he did not stop practicing. Because he had passion, he practiced harder than any other player on the court. He had a vision that defined his future and how he wanted the world to remember him. Vision is the only way to achieve true success and to have true vision is to have true passion. You must always be honing your craft and learning everything there is to know about it. Measure what you are doing right and what you are doing wrong so you can avoid repeating costly mistakes and continue to move forward.

Sacrifice

Sacrifice can be defined as doing selfless good deeds without expecting anything in return. True sacrifice will only happen when you love something so much that you will do anything for it. Sacrificing for someone else's betterment is true sacrifice. Every day millions of parents sacrifice for their children in the form of college savings. They put off buying new cars or home entertainment systems so that their children can have an opportunity at a better future. You don't have to give up all of your earthly possessions and become a missionary in order to make a difference; it's the small things we do on a regular basis that matter the most.

A few days ago as I was driving home from work, I saw two young men with sign that read "Traveling missionaries in need of help; will work for food and gas." In the past, I would have not paid much attention to them. I used to think that anyone asking for handouts was lazy and didn't deserve any pity because they were choosing not to work like the rest of us. As I matured, I realized that I didn't want to be that guy who never helped people around him and once my mission became clear, it went against every part of my being not to help them.

Sure, it is easy to sacrifice for my wife and children, but much harder to sacrifice for people on the side of the road. I never want to look at my life and remember times that I didn't try to help others. What may be a few dollars to me may mean the world to someone in a desperate situation. Give it a try. The next time someone is in need, bend over backwards for him or her, or aid in their rescue. Trust me; you'll get so much joy and satisfaction out of helping others that you may become addicted to it.

Sacrifice doesn't always have to be painful. Remember that small lifestyle changes can make a tremendous difference to others. In Africa, 40 cents a day can bring someone suffering from AIDS medical treatment. Now, not getting your cup of joe once a week isn't a huge sacrifice, but the five bucks a week that you decided to give up and donated means a whole lot for someone. "Caritas Christi" means love as Christ loved, serve as Christ served. We put this Latin saying on the foundation of our new medical building because it is our mission to do exactly that.

Focus

"Concentrate all your thoughts upon the work at hand. The sun's rays do not burn until brought to a focus."

—Alexander Graham Bell

Violet Beauregard from *Willy Wonka and the Chocolate Factory* is a classic example of a character with focus. Throughout the course of the movie, you can hear her parents constantly reminding the young girl to keep her "eye on the prize." In the context of the film, the concept of focus is dramatically overblown, but not by much. The ability to stay fixated on a goal is the true essence of focus. True focus is only achieved when you block out all of the clutter that is preventing you from achieving your goals. In the end, you should fight to stay in line with your goals no matter what the circumstances. This laser sharp focus is all that separates sports stars from mediocre players. Superstars always get that ball in the hoop or make that touchdown because they can shut out any noise that distracts them from their goals.

It can seem overwhelming some days to do anything other than "survive." The more focused you become and the closer you get to uncovering your purpose, the less overwhelming such excellence becomes. Try to simplify your life as much as possible to make more time for what is truly important. In the end, you should always make decisions in line with your goals, no matter what the circumstances may be. This can be difficult, but it is necessary in order to really stay focused and on course. We won't be on this earth forever! Having a ferocious, single minded focus makes you ultra effective.

"When you focus on being a blessing, God makes sure that you are always blessed in abundance."

—Joel Osteen

Six steps to sharpening your focus:

1. **Get rid of static and distractions, including the negative people in your life**: Instead of working at a job you hate, work at finding one that you are passionate about or one that is at least in the field that excites you. There is nothing wrong with starting at the very bottom, but at least do so in a line of business about which you are passionate. If you work hard, you should eventually move on to something a little further up that ladder. Remember, every single thing that you do must be in line with your goals.

2. **Don't neglect your physical needs**: I mentioned the importance of nutrition and proper sleep in a previous chapter, but it is imperative to keep that as a priority to stay focused. No one can be at their best living on caffeine and sugar.

These cause mood swings and crashes in energy that will slow you down and keep your mind fuzzy.

3. **If you keep your focus in line with your purpose, it will be much harder for you to go off track throughout the course of your journey**: Your ultimate life's mission will provide constant support against any possible storms.

4. **Stay educated**: Read books that inspire you and encourage you to better yourself. Listen to your favorite authors on your iPod or in your car. Keep yourself motivated by listening to great motivational speakers.

5. **Spend time in nature**: There is a calming, restorative quality to being outside. Use your time there to brainstorm, visualize, and make goals for yourself or just allow your brain to rest. Some of the best ideas come during downtime.

6. **Exercise!** There is no getting around how exercise is vital to good focus. There is nothing like a good sweat to clear your head, get your priorities in line, and help

you recognize the big picture. You could combine numbers five and six by taking a walk or jog outside.

Going the Extra Mile

Jesus spent his life focused on the concept of servitude. He demonstrated this belief by selfless acts such as washing the feet of his disciples and ultimately sacrificing himself. Jesus taught that there is no greater gift than bringing joy to other people. Giving your life away and becoming a true servant, though often difficult, leads to great rewards because of the positive differences you can make in the lives of others.

By simply focusing on servitude and "going the extra mile," you can exemplify excellence and accumulate wealth. People are drawn to those who practice what they preach. In business, if you go above and beyond what a customer expects of you, you will retain that client for life. A mechanic who not only fixes a car, but also washes it, will have a greater chance at success than a mechanic who returns the car to the customer just as dirty as it was when they dropped it off. Remember that you always get what you give. If you give more than what is required, you will get more than you expected.

Discipline

"In reading the lives of great men, I found that the first victory they won was over themselves. Self-discipline with all of them came first."

—Harry S. Truman

Discipline means staying focused on your goals without distractions. You don't have to worry as much about bad habits when you have discipline because it keeps you on track. Discipline takes time to develop and requires constant sacrifice and dedication. To become more disciplined, you must be able to take constructive criticism from yourself and others. You need to be able to look at yourself, measure what needs to change, and take action based on what you see. Discipline and focus go hand in hand.

Persistence

Being persistent is having the ability to continue trying, even when the outlook is grim and the results aren't much better. Without persistence, a lot of guys I know would still be single! Without persistence and discipline, achievement is impossible. As persistence always has a positive or negative goal at the end of it, it is important that you recognize and pursue the correct type of persistence. It's important to be able to determine which activities are worth your time that day, and be persistent and diligent about those chosen things.

Make yourself a student of time management, and use it to your advantage. You can have the greatest goal in the world but if you are not active in achieving it, you will never succeed. Activity is not an accomplishment in and of itself. If you're always active, but in the wrong direction, or in too many activities at once, you will never achieve goals. You may be "busy," but you're still broke! Persistence doesn't just happen, but develops day by day and demands faith in what you're doing. It takes a total belief in what you're trying to accomplish to have sufficient persistence for the long haul. It is important to use that focus we discussed, since your ability to be persistent determines your level of effectiveness and achievement.

Why is failure important?

There is nothing wrong with failure as long as you learn from it and move on. Persistence will eventually turn failures into success anyway, but only if you are unwilling to give up just because you made a mistake. It is critical to learn from failure. This learning can be achieved through self-reflection, which is one of the most important tools in life, because it prevents mistakes from repeating themselves while it helps foster growth.

At the office, I tell my employees that they are doing great work and inspire them to be better people. People who are encouraged and inspired are more likely to respond positively. To see areas in which you can improve, it is critical to take constructive criticism to heart and really consider the areas where you can perform differently. Instead of reacting defensively and reflexively, try not to respond to criticism immediately. Instead, stay quiet and only respond after some honest reflection on what was said.

To avoid future failure, engage in peer reviews at work and hold family meetings at home. Ask your peers and family members to tell you honestly what you are doing right and what you can do differently. Understand how you can change to better accommodate the people around you, rather than expecting them to change. Remember, this will make you better at what you choose to do, and a more well-rounded person in general.

Chapter 11

Financial Wellness

"If you are going to think anyway, you might as well think big!"

—Donald Trump

Financial Wellness

What does financial wellness mean?

Financial wellness is **your ability to go out and make something from nothing. It depends entirely on your ability to provide something that is going to be of enough value to someone so that he or she is willing to pay you for it.** Contrary to popular belief, financial wellness does not depend on how much money you have in your bank account. You will never have financial wellness or freedom just because you have a large balance. Instead, financial wellness comes from your earning power and understanding how to execute the actions necessary to create wealth.

What is money?

Money is nothing more than a green piece of paper used as a medium of exchange. Before money was invented, society adhered to the barter system. If one person needed meat and another person needed vegetables, the two parties would work out a fair exchange. As commerce started to increase and more items became available on the market, it became that much harder to determine a fair exchange between two very different objects. For the sake of convenience, money was invented as a medium of exchange to make trade easier. If you see money as nothing more than a bargaining tool, you will stop giving it more power than it actually has. This mental shift will change your perception of money and your ability to earn. You will begin to understand that if you start to provide better products or services for someone else, money will be an automatic byproduct of this exchange.

Why is money such a big deal?

Traditionally, money is often perceived as something negative; yet it still continues to dominate our thoughts. The truth is, money is important and it is a big deal because without it you simply do not have the same choices in life. To provide for yourself and your family, get an education, buy a house, travel, or anything else, you need money. Many people justify that money is not important because they do not have it. So why is money such a big deal or, in most cases, a big problem for so many people?

Conditioning

The root of every problem is bad conditioning. Whether you are aware of it or not, you believe what you do because of the way you were conditioned. From birth, each of us is influenced environmentally, mentally, and socially by our own parents, teachers, friends, pastors, TV, and other factors.

Examine the ways that you may have been financially conditioned. Was money openly talked about in your household? Was it off-limits? What were your financial conditions while growing up? Unless you made a conscious choice to change any bad conditioning you may have toward money, you will always carry that with you. Ultimately, this attitude will prevent you from ever being in a positive financial situation. Most people never take control over their conditioning and rely on excuses. To overcome any animosity you may have towards money, start by asking yourself how your parents and family influenced you, and connect those influences back to your present financial condition. Once you find that connection, you can start to change your financial blueprint and head toward a brighter financial future.

Playing the Victim

Most people are victims. We want to say money is not important but it dominates our thoughts on a daily basis. We think about it dozens and dozens of times a day, regardless of whether those thoughts are good or bad. Most people are victims because they perceive money as something they do not have control over. They believe they need to go to work to perform a job and make a certain amount. They need an education, they need to be loyal, and depend on someone else to give them a promotion so they can get ahead.

All of these beliefs may be valid, but they simply feed the victim mindset. In order to obtain a mastery mindset, you need to take full responsibility for yourself and the amount of money you earn. Do not let your lifestyle depend on how much money you have. Instead, figure out the type of lifestyle you want and then go find a way to earn enough money to pay for it.

How Do I Earn More Money?

> *"Formal education will make you a living; self-education will make you a fortune."*
>
> **—Jim Rohn**

When you read this subtitle, pay particular attention to the word ***earn***. You do not make money. You earn money. As previously discussed, money is a medium of exchange in which you need to create enough value through a product or service so that someone wants to trade with you. So how exactly can you earn more money?

1. **Trade time for money**: Trading time for money is a strategy followed by 95% of the population. Unfortunately, it doesn't work because you are still depending on someone to support your lifestyle. Eventually you will run out of time and reach an earnings cap. The American system of higher education feeds into this mentality by conditioning us to think that we will earn more if we continue to get more education, while in fact we are continuing to trade time for money.

2. **Trade money to earn money**: Trading money to earn money is the most technical method through which to earn money, which is done by only 3% of the entire population. The problem with this technique is that you need money to start earning money as well as a specialized knowledge of financial markets and investments. To overcome the technical aspect, you can hire a dedicated professional, but you still need to have some understanding. In order to control of your financial future, you never want to delegate your investments fully to someone else. As demonstrated by the

Bernie Madoff scandal, leaving all of your finances in the hands of someone else can lead to disaster.

3. **Multiply your time by setting up multiple sources of income**: Having multiple streams of income for which you take a creative or productive role allows you to leverage yourself and substantially increase your earning power. The phrase "I'd rather earn 1% from a hundred people than 100% by myself" demonstrates the power of having a proper team and using strategies that will allow you to earn and maintain stability in any market. Truly wealthy people leverage themselves through different business investments and multiples sources of income.

What is the formula for wealth?

1. **The amount of money we earn is dictated by the demand for what we do**: In order to earn money, there has to be a need for what you do. An idea can be creative and exciting but will never go far if there is no need for it.

2. **Ability to execute**: Your ability to provide a service that fills a need in the marketplace, which allows you to leverage your skills and knowledge, is a crucial aspect in the formula for wealth. Your ability to do whatever you do must be developed on a daily basis. Once you become a true professional at what you do, you own your skill and earn money regardless of location or economic conditions. Find your strength and work on developing it and expanding it every day.

3. **Difficulty of replacing**: This is directly related to number two. If you are a true expert in your field, you will be irreplaceable. Your clients will not be able to go down the street and get the same service for a cheaper rate because of the value you provide. As you get better, you will become more difficult to replace and your fees will get higher, thus increasing your earning power.

4. **Scale or quantity**: The scale or quantity on which you deliver a product or service will determine the amount of money you earn. You should consider this factor from

the very start of your financial path. If you want to remain local, you have to realize that you will not earn as much as you would if you operated globally. In order to earn more and become successful on a global scale, you need to be very skilled at what you do. Skill will determine the amount of money you earn.

As stated in the beginning of this chapter, financial wellness has nothing to do with your bank balance but everything to do with your ability to create value. In order to earn money, you need to develop and sell your ideas, products, and services. How well you are able to do this determines your power to earn money. In order to stop playing the role of victim and start taking control of your financial future, you must take responsibly by following your passion, learning how to create value from that interest, and leveraging that value on a global scale.

"Money was never a big motivation for me, except as a way to keep score. The real excitement is playing the game."

—Donald Trump

Entrepreneurship is the True Key to Financial Freedom.

We all know of famous entrepreneurs, people who became famous through their wealth and business success. Just think of Andrew Carnegie, Howard Hughes, John D. Rockefeller, Richard Branson, Jean Paul Getty, Steve Jobs and Oprah Winfrey. Moguls and tycoons, they are people who built empires from their businesses and thrived. They are the envy of the common folk, but as per the definition of an entrepreneur they took great risk for the potential of great reward.

Many of these famous entrepreneurs were not born great, but achieved greatness through their business savvy and indomitable entrepreneurial spirit. They are a financial inspiration for the rest of us and by studying their lives and methods we might learn valuable lessons regarding wealth and success. If they were not born great, what is it that made them great? Is there something that they all have in common or does each have his or her own unique disposition?

Whether they achieved their wealth through oil like Rockefeller or computer software like Bill Gates, they all had their fair share of trials and tribulations to overcome. Here are some valuable "nuggets" as I like to call them, ideas of "gold" that can be learned from their struggles and how they overcame them:

Do they act a certain way towards others? Do they see the world in the same way that we do or is there something radically different? These famous entrepreneurs may have something valuable to teach us and if we take a look at how these individuals lived we will have immeasurable knowledge about what it takes to achieve financial greatness.

As I have studied these individuals I have concluded that they were all human with faults and weaknesses, but what intrigues me is how they over came them and achieved financial independence. I set out to learn as much as I can about each and every one of them and then to use their methods, ideas, and techniques in my own life as an entrepreneur and see if it would help me in my personal struggle for financial freedom.

The sheer size of the achievements of these famous entrepreneurs is inspiring to me. After studying them I hoped to gain a better understanding of what it takes to become finically independent. Each of them shared the same quality in that they believed in what they were selling. They weren't being mendacious when selling a prospective new client.

"When fate hands you a lemon,
make lemonade."

—Dale Carnegie

My Questions to You Are:

1. **Do you enjoy what you do?** All of these individuals fell in love with what they did.

2. **Do you believe in what you do?** Each one of them truly believed in the product they were selling whether it was an idea or a commodity.

At the end of the day if you answered yes and you don't find financial freedom will you be happy to have known that you tried? As they say, "It's better to have tried and failed than to not have tried at all." It is important in your persistent quest for financial freedom not to forget about your health, because if you don't have your health you have nothing at all.

"So many people spend their health gaining wealth, and then have to spend their wealth to regain their health."

—Jackie Mason

About the Author

Dr. Unruh received his Doctorate of Chiropractic Degree from the Cleveland College of Chiropractic in Los Angeles, CA. He has also invested nearly 400 hours of study in post graduate work in subject areas including: low back pain, traumatic brain and spine injuries and auto crash reconstruction.

Dr. Unruh is the founder of the Unruh Spine Center, a multi-disciplinary medical/natural health center. His center takes both an eastern and western approach to healthcare bringing relief to patients that was not previously available.

He resides in Southern California with his wife and three beautiful children.